Feeding Hungry People

RULEMAKING IN THE FOOD STAMP PROGRAM

JEFFREY M. BERRY

Feeding Hungry People

RULEMAKING IN THE FOOD STAMP PROGRAM

Rutgers University Press
New Brunswick, New Jersey

Library of Congress Cataloging in Publication Data

Berry, Jeffrey M., 1948–
    Feeding hungry people.

    Includes index.
    1. Food stamp program—United States—History.
    2. Food stamp program—Government policy—
    United States. I. Title.
    HV696.F6B47   1984   363.8'82'0973   83–8712
    ISBN 0–8135–1013–9

To Lori

CONTENTS

TABLES

ACKNOWLEDGMENTS

Much of the research for this study was done through interviews with major participants in food stamp policy making. Elite (nonstandardized) interviews were conducted with congressmen, legislative aides, career civil servants and political appointees in the Department of Agriculture, Office of Management and Budget officials, White House staffers, and lobbyists. The forty or so interviews were generally granted on a not-for-attribution basis. All of the unattributed quotations in the text come from these interviews. I am indebted to all of the individuals who gave so willingly of their time.

Another major source of data for this study came from Department of Agriculture and White House files. Scholars are fortunate that the Department of Agriculture has a sense of its past. It employs a group of professional historians who gave me access to files preserved from the Kennedy and Johnson years. These files are not, however, organized in a systematic manner, and most of the documents I used from this collection are cited here as belonging to the "History Group Files." More recent department files were provided by the secretary of agriculture's office. I was also able to examine files in the Lyndon Baines Johnson Library at the University of Texas. Documents from the LBJ Library can be found under the name of the author of the memorandum cited. I thank all the people at the Department of Agriculture and the LBJ Library who were so helpful to me in the course of my research.

This book could not have been written without a generous grant from the Ford Foundation, which allowed me to spend a year in Washington doing field research. I deeply appreciate the opportunity afforded me by Ford's Government and Law program. During the year I spent in Washington, the Brookings Institution graciously provided me with guest scholar privileges. A Moody Grant from the Lyndon B. Johnson Foundation enabled me to travel to Austin, Texas, to use the LBJ Library. The Tufts Faculty Fund was kind enough to give me a summer grant to continue the work on this project.

While doing the research and writing for this study, I sought the advice of many individuals. I thank Martha Derthick, Jerry Goldman, Barbara Kellerman, Barry Mitnick, Richard Nathan, Kent Portney, Paul Schulman, and Gilbert Steiner for their help. Michael Hayes and A. Lee Fritschler, who read the manuscript for Rutgers University Press, offered me many valuable suggestions. At Rutgers Press, Marlie Wasserman was a helpful and encouraging editor. I also thank Deborah Manning for her assistance in typing the manuscript.

During the years it took to complete this study, my wife, Lori, was a constant source of support. This book is dedicated to her.

ABBREVIATIONS

AFDC	Aid to Families with Dependent Children
CNI	Community Nutrition Institute
FAP	Family Assistance Plan
FNS	Food and Nutrition Service
FRAC	Food Research and Action Center
HEW	Department of Health, Education, and Welfare
HUD	Department of Housing and Urban Development
OMB	Office of Management and Budget
USDA	Department of Agriculture

Feeding Hungry People

RULEMAKING IN THE FOOD STAMP PROGRAM

Introduction

SOCIAL POLICY AND THE REGULATORY CONTEXT

FEW ASPECTS OF AMERICAN society have been left untouched by the regulations of federal administrative agencies. There are regulations to cover everything from day care centers to funeral homes. Most of the regulations that come out of Washington each week have little impact on the consciousness of the general public. Yet regulations affect the quality of life of ordinary citizens. They are not the mere details of public policy.

The food stamp program is a case in point. During the life of the program, crucial decisions have time and time again been made through the rulemaking process. Regulations set forth by the Department of Agriculture (USDA) have helped to determine who is eligible for food stamps. Regulations created the initial benefit structure for recipients. The amount of coupons available to each family has repeatedly been altered by changes in program regulations. Regulations have been used to put more individuals on to the program and to remove others' eligibility, to give some recipients more coupons and to give others fewer.

Sometimes USDA made these policy decisions through rulemaking because members of Congress were generally apathetic about the program. It was policy making by default. At other times USDA had to act because the Congress was split over what changes needed to be made. Vague statutory language often papered over deep-seated disagreement between liberal and conservative legislators. In such cases program administrators untangled the congressional compromise and made the substantive policy decision. In still other cases USDA made policy decisions through regulations even though the Congress did not want it to do so. The result was conflict over how much authority Congress had delegated to the department.

1

Throughout its history, the food stamp program has been the focus of repeated clashes over how much responsibility USDA should have in setting program policy. On one level, this question may seem to be an abstract issue of interest primarily to scholars who study the separation of powers or congressional-bureaucratic relations. On another level, the question has much more immediate significance: For the impoverished recipients of food stamps, these decisions determine how much food will go on the table.

THE REGULATORY PROCESS

Food stamps is but one of countless domestic programs that utilize administrative regulations. Each agency must use its regulatory powers to transform statutes into practical rules for program implementation. Regulations must be written so as to maximize both program effectiveness and political acceptability.

The broad goal of the present work is to expand what we know about the role of regulations in the development of social policy. How do administrators actually reach regulatory decisions? How do members of Congress try to control the content of regulations? In what ways do interest groups, public opinion, and the White House influence the formation of regulations? Using the food stamp program as a source of data, I shall attempt to increase our understanding of how regulations are written.

Regulations cannot be divorced from their larger political context. They are part of the struggle over who gets what—and how much—from our government. Proposed regulations, like proposed legislation, are the focal point for the clash of interests in a society. Research on regulations and social policy may help us to learn more about congressional-agency relations, legislative and administrative behavior, and interest group advocacy. But underlying all the empirical questions is a more practical concern: How might the process of writing regulations be reformed to improve governmental policy making?

"Regulation" is a term commonly used to describe any type of administrative decision that sets forth agency policy. In a legal sense, regulations are those agency policies that have been fashioned through specified administrative procedures under direct grants of statutory authority. Administrative rulemaking is a method of formulating regulations in a quasi-legislative manner. The regulations issued apply to the general public and have the force of law. Rulemaking is governed by the Administrative Procedure Act (1946), which directs agencies to promote open and systematic consideration of their rules.[1]

Rulemaking usually proceeds in the following manner. When an agency is faced with a policy question that falls within its delegated authority, it must ascertain whether a rule of general applicability is warranted. If this is the case, agency staff members will draft a regulation after reviewing all available data. Sometimes public hearings will take place early in the drafting of a regulation, so that more information may be gathered. Once a draft regulation is approved by the responsible agency officials, it is published in its proposed form in the *Federal Register*, which contains all proposed and final regulations of government agencies. The *Federal Register* is published each weekday, and roughly sixty thousand copies are distributed to libraries, the Congress, government offices, private organizations, and interested individuals.

After a proposed regulation appears, the public has an opportunity to "comment" on it. Before an agency makes a final decision on its regulation, it must weigh the sentiments expressed in the letters it has received. The agency may even schedule hearings at this stage to permit concerned parties to make oral arguments on the proposed regulation. Finally, the agency will decide whether to adopt its rule—in its original or modified form—or to drop the proposed regulation altogether. If a regulation is adopted, it is again published in the *Federal Register*. All the regulations of the government are compiled into volumes of the *Code of Federal Regulations*.

Regulations may arise out of any one of three sources. First, a statute may be passed by the Congress which grants an agency or department the authority to prepare accompanying regulations. Second, regulations may have to be written because of a court case. A court's decision may invalidate existing regulations or require an agency to generate regulations where none exists. Third, regulations may come about because of internal review. When the operation or implementation of a program reveals problems with ongoing policy, administrators respond by redesigning program rules.

The degree to which government should set policy through the regulatory process is an enduring question of American politics. To what extent should government decisions be made by agencies rather than by Congress? Since the very beginning of this country, Congress has had to delegate authority to executive branch departments.[2] The practical dictates of policy making meant that Congress could not deal with all the decisions of government that had to be made each day. Moreover, as government grew and policies became more complex, the specialized expertise that administrators could offer was a further reason for delegating authority. Delegation also allowed for flexibility in policy, giving administrators the means to adopt policies as needed, without having to resort to the slow and cumbersome legislative process.

Few critics would disagree that it is necessary for administrators to make numerous policy decisions if government is to function with reasonable efficiency. Still, regulations, as instruments of social and economic policy, have probably never been as unpopular as they are today. Regulations have come to represent the evils of big government. They are so numerous, so detailed, and so ever present that they are regarded as symbolic of a government that tries to do too much. Regulations have also come to represent the complexity of public policy and the distance between government and the common man.[3] They are so hard to read that one is tempted to believe that lawyers have conspired to make them so, creating a whole new business for themselves: explaining regulations to clients.

The dissatisfaction with excessive regulation by government cuts across all groups and ideological persuasions. For businessmen, it may be the Occupational Safety and Health Administration's regulations on the design of exit signs or its standards for portable wooden ladders that are most irksome. For consumers, the rulings of economic regulatory agencies that act to lessen business competition seem contrary to the nature of capitalism. For any citizen, the red tape of applying for welfare or a government-sponsored loan can be an exasperating experience.

President Ronald Reagan has pledged his administration to a program of large-scale deregulation. In a number of areas affecting business markets, the administration has revised regulatory standards in an effort to reduce the government's policing role, to increase capital formation, and to stimulate competition. The president's approach to domestic policy programs for income maintenance, social services, education, economic development, and the like is even more far-reaching. His philosophy advocates turning over control of these programs to state and local governments. During his first year in office, Reagan proposed that funds for many programs be lumped together into a small number of block grants that the states and cities would control. The block grant plans achieved mixed results in the Congress; some were enacted into law while others were quietly tabled.

In his State of the Union Address at the start of his second year in office, Reagan continued to press for the transfer of domestic programs away from the federal government. Under Reagan's initial "New Federalism" plan, the states and cities would take over food stamps, Aid to Families with Dependent Children (AFDC), and forty-three smaller programs, while the federal government would assume full responsibility for Medicaid and would give the states some additional sources of revenue. When the proposal met stiff opposition from the nation's governors, the White House tried to placate them by dropping the food stamp transfer. Although the prospects for an omnibus New Federalism plan are problematic, it seems clear that the Reagan administration will push for greater state and local authority over domestic policy programs for as long as it is in office. The sum and substance of block grants and the New Federalism is that national standards are replaced by state and local preferences.

REGULATIONS AS SOCIAL POLICY

Given the importance of regulations in the formulation of public policy, it is not surprising that political scientists and economists have conducted extensive research on an almost endless variety of regulated industries and their governing agencies. These studies have emphasized the effects of regulation and the theories behind regulatory activity. Another major area of focus has been the legislative environment. Vague enabling legislation and inadequate oversight have been found to be common congressional responses to regulatory problems.

Out of this rich and valuable literature has come a sophisticated body of knowledge concerning the regulatory process.[4] Yet our knowledge of governmental regulation remains limited. The research up to now has been devoted almost exclusively to economic regulations.[5] Nonetheless, regulation by the federal government encompasses a far wider range of activities than determining standards, rates, and fair practices for different segments of the economy. It is important to extend research on the regulatory process to such nonmarket policy areas as nutrition, mental health, job training, community development, cash assistance, and social insurance.

Of course, the agencies that regulate economic interests differ significantly from those that have responsibility for social welfare programs. Social welfare agencies do not divide up markets among competitors; they are not structured as independent commissions; and they do not appear to have well-organized clients. Still, there is one basic similarity between social and economic regulatory agencies that must not be overlooked: Both types of agencies have been given authority by Congress to allocate goods and services among the American people. Every agency that has been given rulemaking powers must interpret congressional intent and then make discretionary decisions as to what policies best serve the public's needs.

If more is to be learned about regulations and social policy, individual programs must be examined in great detail. Rulemaking can be fully understood only with a solid background in program operation. When I began this study, I felt strongly that Washington-based field research was needed to illuminate the subtle and complex nature of the rulemaking process. The public record, such as it exists, simply does not explain what goes on during the writing of program regulations. As one of this country's most widely used and best known forms of welfare, the food stamp program provided an excellent basis for an inquiry of this sort.

One of the advantages of the lengthy case study that follows is that it offers the opportunity to trace changes in the rulemaking process over a period of roughly twenty years. Some of the controversies surrounding program regulations have lasted for a decade or more. An additional value of this chronological treatment of the food stamp program is that it affords a chance to observe the long-term evolution of specific policy issues. The varying administrative responses to these issues can thus be surveyed as part of this investigation.

Although there are few studies on Congress, agencies, and social policy rulemaking, political scientists have debated many similar problems in related contexts. This work draws principally on four areas of political science as its base for examining the regulatory process for food stamps. In each of these areas (to be discussed below), prevailing generalizations in the literature guided my research. Testing such generalizations serves two purposes. First, it contributes to the systematic development of our knowledge about the political process. Individual propositions must be subjected to careful analysis if theory building is to proceed. Second, evaluating this literature in light of a lengthy case study facilitates realistic consideration of alternatives for reforming the process. The seemingly universal criticism of the role that administrative agencies play in making policy is not matched by agreement over what should be done to improve agency rulemaking.

LEGISLATIVE BEHAVIOR

Few subfields of political science are as rich as that of legislative behavior. The literature abounds with studies of how and why congressmen behave the way they do. Their voting patterns, propensity to join coalitions, committee work, constituency relations, and other activities have been explored in detail. Less is known about their dealings with agency administrators and staff, and their role in administrative rulemaking has been largely ignored.

This study begins with the simple premise that congressmen actively try to influence the content of administrative regulations. Statute writing and regulation writing are not two separate processes. Policy making involves ongoing interaction between legislators and administrators. The issuance of regulations can prompt legislative conflict, cause Congress to rethink its intent, and stimulate congressional efforts to curb administrative discretion.[6]

In very broad terms, there are two means by which legislators influence the content of regulations. The first, and most obvious, is through the way they write and rewrite legislation. In trying to accomplish their policy goals, members of the authorizing committees are concerned with the language of bills and with the content of legislative reports. The legislative reports that accompany bills passed by committees elaborate on congressional thinking and give additional information to the administrators who must try to gauge Congress's intent.[7] A critical juncture in Congress's efforts to influence agency regulations takes place when a program comes up for reauthorization or is being amended for other reasons. When existing legislation is formally reviewed, a de facto review of existing regulations also occurs. Policy decisions embodied in regulations can be considered anew if congressmen disagree over them. Indeed, much of what a congressional committee does in amending a law is to put into statute their revisions of previously issued regulations.

A second method of influencing the content of regulations is intervention in the rulemaking process. When an agency is considering new rules to be proposed, congressmen may directly attempt to sway administrators toward making a particular choice. This effort may be undertaken publicly, with congressmen using the media or some other means to draw attention to a pending or newly issued regulation. In the history of the food stamp program, a favorite tactic of intervention has been the holding of congressional hearings. Program supporters have used the hearings to publicize regulations that seemed harsh in their impact on recipients.

Private intervention into rulemaking, though out of the public eye, is not necessarily secretive. Letters, phone calls, and meetings with administrators are some of the means used by legislators to add further guidance to Congress's intent as embodied in a statute. Intervention is like any other form of political bargaining. Coalitions are built, resources are allocated in a judicious fashion, and negotiators push toward compromise when the opposing parties seem willing to bargain. Legislative intervention into rulemaking is an everyday activity in Washington;[8] yet it is virtually ignored in most texts and scholarly treatments of the public policy-making process.

A third method of influencing agency rulemaking was through the formal clearance of regulations. The legislative veto, which gave Congress the right to overturn regulations without having to amend the relevant law, rose in popularity in the past decade. More and more laws embodied legislative vetoes in a variety of forms. Ruling in an immigration case in June 1983, however, the Supreme Court struck down the legislative veto because it did not conform with the framers' intent for the enactment of legislation.

In analyzing the efforts of congressmen to influence the regulatory process, a fundamental question emerges: Why do congressmen expend valuable resources (their time and energy) on detailed, complicated issues that are typically of low salience? A prevailing view of legislative behavior, outlined by David Mayhew in *Congress: The Electoral Connection*, is that congressmen are single-minded seekers of re-election.[9] As such, they will allocate their time and resources toward those activities that will do them the most good at election time. Intervention into bureaucratic policy making would seem to be far down the list of activities that are beneficial in this way. Only when there is much credit to be claimed does intervention make sense for the electorally motivated congressman. Since the rulemaking process generally lacks any significant visibility, congressmen will usually find it much easier to gain publicity if they spend their time campaigning and doing other parts of their job.

In line with the thinking of Mayhew and others, Congress's limited oversight can be explained by the lack of incentives. Yet oversight studies tend to ignore informal intervention into rulemaking and thus discount what may be a significant part of Congress's efforts to see that the programs created by its laws are implemented correctly.[10] Congress is roundly condemned for its unwillingness to take responsibility for consistent oversight. Nonetheless, in the case of the food stamp program a small number of congressmen have in fact actively intervened to move USDA to follow the law's intent.

It may well be that the incentive system for congressmen is grossly oversimplified by assuming that there is little reason for them to get involved in less glamorous, less visible work like intervening in agency rulemaking. A major purpose of this book will be to reassess this assumption. How does legislative intervention into administrative rulemaking change or reinforce our theoretical understanding of what motivates congressmen?

INTEREST GROUP ADVOCACY

Traditionally, the most impoverished individuals in American society—including the clients of the food stamp program—have had little direct interest group representation in the governmental process. The development of the food stamp program coincides, however, with the growth of the public interest movement. Over time, citizen groups have come to play an increasingly active role in trying to influence food stamp policy.

The rise of citizen advocacy during the late 1960s and 1970s was greeted by many as a sign of democratic renewal.[11] As new groups formed to push for changes in areas such as civil rights, environmental regulation, and consumer protection, constituencies that had never been effectively organized were brought into the policy-making process. Government, in turn, responded with many new laws and regulatory agencies. America seemed to be regaining the ideal of participatory democracy, a welcome development given the conflict and alienation of the times.

Yet, for some, the increase in citizen advocacy has been a cause for concern. Most prominent among the critics is political scientist Samuel Huntington, who has warned against an "excess of democracy."[12] In Huntington's eyes, the wave of new citizen lobbies produced by the "democratic surge" of the 1960s "overloaded" the political system. The expansion of governmental activity could not possibly satisfy all competing demands, and, ultimately, the authority of government was undermined. Increased participation made the nation less governable.

More specific criticisms have been directed at citizen groups as well. They have been accused of creating unnecessary and costly delays in the development of much-needed housing, water, and energy-related projects. They have been accused of insensitivity toward working-class preferences because the policies they advocate place a higher priority on environmental protection than on job protection. Most recently, citizen groups have come under attack for helping to fracture America into single-issue constituencies.[13]

Prior to the civil rights and antiwar movements, citizen lobbies received little serious coverage in the standard texts on interest groups and were treated as anomalies in more sophisticated, theoretical works. In *The Logic of Collective Action*, economist Mancur Olson showed why it is irrational in most instances for an individual to join a voluntary organization to support its lobbying efforts.[14] Even though a person may be very much in favor of a group's political goals, he or she can be a "free rider" by enjoying whatever lobbying victories the organization earns without having to pay any dues. Nevertheless, public interest groups, which seek "collective goods" and ideological rewards without selectively and materially benefiting members, exist in defiance of the free rider logic.[15] Most of these groups are disproportionately composed of upper-middle-class professionals who can more easily afford the luxury of paying to support such organizations.

For groups that focus on welfare issues, however, the problems of organizing are exacerbated by the indigence of their natural constituents. Moreover, unlike so many environmental and consumer groups, poor people's lobbies have not been able to attract many middle-class patrons. Should the government support welfare advocacy because the interest group "market" has failed to do so? The crucial question is that of representation. Through the 1950s and early 1960s, pluralists argued that public policy was the product of bargaining between government and interest groups. Although pluralism has become discredited as fact, it nevertheless remains desirable as a *goal*. But if interest groups are generally skewed toward middle-class interests, how can the unrepresented be brought to the bargaining table?

To promote pluralism in welfare policy making, the federal government has relied on two major approaches. The first has been various grant-in-aid programs. Activists at the local, state, and national levels have received money for training, community organizing, education, and direct advocacy. A second method has been citizen participation programs. Many agencies are required to form advisory boards, hold hearings, or use some other forum to elicit the views of those affected by pending projects or regulations.[16]

Though liberals remain convinced that government must continue actively to encourage representation of welfare interests in its policy making, there is no agreement as to which approach works best. This is an increasingly relevant policy question, since the Reagan administration is reducing support for both direct grants and citizen participation. Conservatives question whether government has any responsibility to ensure that different interests are independently represented before policy-making bodies. Even if expanded public participation in politics is desirable in theory, is it (as Huntington argues) counterproductive in practice?

The analysis here will begin by trying to gauge the impact of citizen advocacy on food stamp policy making. What are the costs and benefits of public involvement in policy making? An examination of the effects of citizen advocacy on USDA rulemaking may reveal how well recipients have been represented and whether or not the administrative process has benefited from government-promoted pluralism.

ISSUE NETWORKS

Political scientists commonly describe Washington politics as subsystem politics. In its simplest form, a policy subsystem consists of a congressional committee or subcommittee, an administrative agency, and relevant interest groups. The terminology has frequently changed, but whether they are called "subgovernments," "iron triangles," or "cozy little triangles," such subsystems are based on the same idea: Agency administrators, lobbyists from client groups, and congressmen with committee jurisdiction over that agency work together continuously to formulate policy.[17]

The policy making in a subsystem is held to be consensual. Each side of the triangle can be helped by working cooperatively with the other two. Congressmen look for political support and campaign contributions from the interest groups. Agency administrators want to protect their budgets and otherwise enhance their programs. Finally, client groups want to make sure that their interests are furthered by government policies. Over time, close working relationships develop, and individuals may even move from one point in the triangle to another, such as the agency official who later takes a job with a client group. It is a "mutual self-help arrangement" where policies are formulated with the needs of all partners in mind.[18]

Subsystem politics has often been criticized as being inimical to the best interests of society. Policies tailored to the requirements of the participants in the various iron triangles may give short shrift to the larger "public interest." There is also a lack of accountability when policies are established through largely informal arrangements by only those friendly to the program at hand. Oversight is neglected in the effort to accommodate the participating interests.

Recently this view of iron triangle subsystems has come under closer scrutiny by political scientists. As Hugh Heclo notes, "The iron triangle concept is not so much wrong as it is disastrously incomplete."[19] Heclo maintains that policy subsystems are much broader and more porous than earlier scholars portrayed them. In addition, many new policy areas have emerged since the original research on iron triangles was done. There has also been a rapid proliferation of interest groups of all kinds, requiring agencies and committees to deal with an increasingly diverse clientele. What Heclo stresses most in comparing contemporary politics with earlier periods during which iron triangles were said to flourish, is that governmental programs are becoming more and more complex. Participation in what Heclo calls "issue networks" is largely based on expertise and technological competence. "Participants move in and out of the networks constantly," he points out, but the key to entering a network is the knowledge one holds about the policy area.[20]

Although Heclo's concept of issue networks is superior to that of iron triangles, there is still a certain amount of vagueness to the whole idea and little concrete knowledge about how issue networks behave. To the question "What does an issue network look like?" Heclo acknowledges that "it is difficult to say precisely. . . ."[21] Moreover, little recent research focuses directly on iron triangles or issue networks. As a result, there is no well-developed set of empirically verified propositions that can form the basis of a theory of issue network politics. Nevertheless, the key assumptions about issue networks are cogent and are expressed forcefully by political scientists. As Dodd and Schott conclude, "power within Washington depends largely on one's ability to influence subsystem politics."[22]

A case study of the food stamp program may offer some insight into issue networks and how they operate. Most thinking about policy subsystems has been formed with farm, labor, or business interests in mind. How might issue networks differ in the area of welfare policy? Welfare client groups, for example, are clearly distinct from those usually described in the literature as being part of policy subsystems. It may be that issue networks vary considerably, depending on the nature of the program in question. Much of the work in policy analysis and policy studies employs typologies that emphasize how distinct policy areas produce distinct policy processes.[23] That type of logic should be applied to issue networks as well.

Research on the food stamp program also allows close examination of how the participants within an issue network interact during the rulemaking process. The previous research on policy subsystems has not focused directly on the writing of regulations, tending to view the overall policy-making process instead. Yet rulemaking is a crucial stage for all three sets of partners, and much of the interaction within an issue network surely takes place when regulations are being written.

ADMINISTRATIVE DISCRETION

Rulemaking must be considered within the context of Congress's constitutional authority to determine the course of domestic policy. The central issue of congressional-agency interaction over regulations is that of legislative control. To what degree should legislators, rather than administrators, determine the "fine print" of public policy? Where is the line that separates the proper legislative role of setting policy guidelines from the proper executive role in administering policy? In theory, this division of labor is based on what is most efficient in terms of legislative time and resources, and what is most practical in terms of administrative experience and expertise. In practice, there is a huge gray area in which the authority of both branches is subject to dispute. At the base of this dispute is the eternal question of separation of powers.

The issue of legislative control can sometimes revolve around the concept of "legislative intent." When Congress, through informal and formal means, tries to give direction to administrative regulations, it is establishing intent. The legal interpretation of intent is based upon the legislative history of a bill that becomes law. The hearings, committee reports, floor debate, and the statute itself are the recorded evidence of congressional intent.[24] The scope of legislative intent, however, often goes beyond what is legally defensible in the courtroom. If statutory provisions are unclear, informal understandings are often reached until more specific guidelines are written into law. However, administrators may choose to interpret ambiguous intent on their own. Likewise, congressmen often intervene to try to persuade administrators of the nature of congressional intent if they feel it has been misinterpreted.

Full legislative control over agency rulemaking can never be gained, not only because administrators must be given some flexibility, but also because Congress is often indecisive or in disagreement over policy. Administrators can be presented with conflicting interpretations of legislative intent when congressmen of opposing views intervene in the rulemaking process. When agency officials use their discretion to choose one policy option over others, they run the risk of angering congressmen who hold contrary opinions. If they offend enough congressmen, the policy may be changed by statute and their own latitude curbed. Thus, although Congress grants agencies the discretion to amplify its policies, those allowances are always tentative and subject to change.

But if full control is neither practical nor desirable, there is still the question of whether Congress goes as far as it should in specifying policy directives to agencies. This problem underlies evaluations of legislative and agency performance. Broadly speaking, two opposing lines of thinking have characterized this debate. One school of thought holds that administrative agencies fail to serve the public interest because they make unwise decisions under grants of excessive discretion. Congress does not sufficiently control the policy making of agencies, either through its authorizing legislation or through legislative oversight. This point of view is represented by such works as Theodore Lowi's *The End of Liberalism.*[25] Lowi concludes that Congress has surrendered its constitutional authority by writing vague legislation that permits agencies to set their own substantive policy. These large grants of discretion lead to agency decisions that are strongly oriented toward the preferences of well-organized interest groups.

In his study of administrative law, Kenneth Culp Davis found the same pattern of legislative failure. Davis contends that Congress has often granted far too much discretion in laws that merely tell agencies, "Here is the problem. Deal with it."[26] A similar theme is sounded by James Q. Wilson. Excessive discretion has made agencies too independent and, consequently, too partial to their clients. The clients, in turn, provide useful political support for the agencies with which they deal. Again, responsibility for this situation lies with the Congress. Wilson notes pessimistically, "Congress could change what it has devised, but there is little reason to suppose it will."[27]

Other scholars, however, have not found agency discretion excessive or administrators generally in need of greater congressional supervision. One of the most forceful statements of this position is Joseph Harris's *Congressional Control of Administration*. Harris defends Congress's grants of significant discretion to administrative agencies: "Effective administration requires that executive officials have appropriate discretion to apply the expertness that they have, but legislatures do not, and to pursue the intent of the law in varying circumstances that legislatures cannot possibly anticipate."[28] Harris is guided by a classical politics/administration dichotomy, where Congress must be watched so that it does not interfere with the more neutral decision making of bureaucrats.

The idea that agency administrators should have substantial discretion by virtue of their expertise runs against the grain of popular dissatisfaction with bureaucratic government. A common complaint is that the bureaucracy is far too independent and far too powerful. On the other hand, Herbert Kaufman has attacked this notion that bureaucracies are "out of control," making policy with relatively few constraints upon them. As Kaufman notes, "strong indicators point to powerful checks on bureaucrats' discretion, limits to their influence, inroads on their independence. On balance, therefore, the case for runaway bureaucracies is no stronger than the case for bridled bureaucracies. . . ."[29]

At one level, the question of control over administrative agencies is a matter of political power. A pre-eminent concern of political scientists has always been to measure the relative levels of influence exerted by participants in the policy-making process. Underlying this question, however, is the notion of accountability. Who, ultimately, is responsible for policies formulated by administrators? Are administrators capable of interpreting the will of the people on their own, or can that will be expressed only through the elected representatives of the people?

This controversy was neatly framed many years ago by the classic exchange of views between Carl Friedrich and Herman Finer. Friedrich argued that the most effective check on administrators is self-restraint.[30] Administrators' technical mastery over their subject matter is such that they must be given considerable discretion—and must therefore be responsible for their actions. In Friedrich's judgment, bureaucrats are responsive to public opinion; in anticipating reactions to their decisions, they take into account the concerns of others when formulating their policies.

Responding to Friedrich, Finer pointed to the potential for abuse of power when self-restraint is the primary check on administrative actions.[31] Administrative responsibility is defined by Finer as the subordination of administrators' views to those of elected officials. To ensure that government functions democratically, strong external controls must be placed on agency officials.

This debate is still relevant today. When agency administrators write regulations, to whom are they accountable? Are external constraints, such as legislative oversight, sufficient to ensure that the will of the people is carried out? Alternatively, does administrative discretion leave agency officials with relative autonomy, permitting them to determine on their own what is in the public interest?

These questions of theory are manifested in the everyday congressional-agency interaction concerning the actual degree of discretion available to administrators, the ways in which oversight of that discretion is carried out, and the manner in which agency officials interpret the intent of Congress. Rulemaking is viewed here as the crux of this relationship. In the case of the food stamp program, was there an optimally effective and rational working relationship between Congress and the Department of Agriculture? More specifically, in the formulation of food stamp regulations did there ever develop a balance between degree of legislative supervision and degree of administrative discretion that, in retrospect, produced the "best" policy decisions?[32]

FOOD STAMPS AS A CASE STUDY

The purpose of the case study that follows is to offer a comprehensive history and analysis of regulation writing for a single program. It is only through in-depth research of this sort that the separate influences that impinge upon rulemaking can be distinguished. The writing of program regulations is rarely covered well by journalists or even by scholars writing about a particular policy problem. The complicated political decisions that lead to specific regulations can be unraveled only if participants are interviewed and if the primary documents are examined.

In choosing a program for study, an effort was made to find one where there had been significant regulatory activity, and where questions had arisen over rulemaking authority. These criteria may have had the effect of biasing the selection toward a program where there has been controversy rather than calm. I believed, however, that the research would be more fruitful if I concentrated on a program where there were problems concerning the discretionary authority of the agency involved. Preliminary research disclosed a history of conflicts over food stamp regulations. In the early years of the program, when most guidelines were not even put through notice and comment, extraordinarily significant decisions were made by administrators who had great discretionary authority.[33] As procedures for writing regulations became more fixed over the years, the discretionary authority open to program officials became a subject of increasing dispute. Throughout the life of the program, regulations have been viewed as fundamental instruments for reforming food stamp policy.

Aside from its bearing on the theoretical problems noted above, the food stamp program is worthy of investigation simply because of its massive size and its importance.[34] It serves as many as 22 million Americans a month, at a cost to the federal government of more than $11 billion for fiscal year 1982. Its clients include those who receive a welfare grant, such as AFDC, as well as those who are not eligible for cash assistance. The food stamp program provides relief to those out of work, whether as a supplement to unemployment compensation or as the sole means of support. Since one out of five food stamp families also receives social security, the program acts as a backup for that system as well.

As it enters its third decade of operation, the food stamp program faces an uncertain future. Under President Reagan's prodding during his first two years in office, the Congress cut over $11 billion from food stamp spending for fiscal years 1982–1985. The program has grown unpopular, and many citizens regard it as too accessible to those who are not really in need. When a 1981 *New York Times*/CBS News poll asked Americans if they favored increased, decreased, or the same level of spending for seven policy areas, the food stamp program was the only one for which a plurality wanted less spending.[35] Clearly, food stamps has lost its positive image as a *feeding* program and gained a negative image as a *welfare* program.

In the four chapters that immediately follow, the history of the food stamp program and the development of its regulations are detailed. The subsequent two chapters place the case study in the larger perspective of legislative, administrative, and interest group behavior.

PART 1

REGULATIONS AND THE DEVELOPMENT OF THE FOOD STAMP PROGRAM

1

A SECOND CHANCE
FOR FOOD STAMPS

L IKE SO MANY OTHER social programs, food stamps originated in New Deal attempts to cope with the Great Depression. The food stamp program was intended to serve more than the poor who would receive the coupons. It was born with the dual purpose of helping farmers as well as the hungry. Without the large crop surpluses in the 1920s and 1930s (and later in the 1950s), it is unlikely that a food stamp system would ever have been considered. The food stamp program was the result of the unsettling contradiction between unprecedented want and deprivation on the one hand and excessive agricultural production on the other.

THE FIRST FOOD STAMP PROGRAM

Although the food stamp program was not inaugurated until 1939, the Roosevelt administration moved in its first year to link relief for the poor to relief for the farmers. The government purchased commodity suprluses and then distributed them to local relief agencies. Packages of these various commodities were in turn given to families in need of assistance. The commodity program proved to be a disappointment because it did not increase demand for farm goods. The poor who received the commodities substituted much of the free food for the items they would otherwise have bought at the grocery store. Early in Roosevelt's second term discussions began on alternatives to the commodity distribution program.[1]

Both Fred Waugh, a USDA economist, and Milo Perkins, head of the Federal Surplus Commodities Corporation, have been popularly credited with thinking up the food stamp program. Both denied that

21

they first conceived the idea. One account places the origins of the program in a conversation during a Sunday drive in the country by Perkins, Secretary of Agriculture Henry Wallace, and their wives.[2] Regardless of its parentage, by 1938 the concept began to receive serious consideration in USDA. The plan that was announced in January 1939 was an imaginative, if cumbersome, means of offering aid to the poor while expanding demand for overabundant commodities. Recipients—families on relief—would purchase orange-colored stamps at the rate of $1.00–1.50 per person per week. The orange stamps would be issued in amounts equivalent to the cash paid in, and they could be used on any item in a grocery store. In addition, for every dollar of orange stamps purchased, recipients would receive a free blue coupon worth fifty cents. These blue coupons could be used to purchase food designated as surplus by the secretary of agriculture. The theory behind the two-color system was that the poor would continue to spend their normal amount on food by means of the orange stamps. Everything purchased with the blue stamps would represent additional buying and, therefore, additional demand for farm goods.

The program was begun in Rochester, New York, in May 1939. Within two years nationwide participation was at a peak of close to 4 million individuals. Before it ended in 1943, almost 1,500 counties had instituted the program, and almost everyone considered it a success. World War II reduced the unemployment and crop surpluses that had made the program necessary and the decision to terminate food stamps met little opposition. The legacy, though, was of a program that had worked. Participants were found to have had a more nutritious diet than nonparticipants at the same income level. And there was an overall increase in food purchasing by recipients, thus providing support for farmers. The one troubling aspect of the program was a perception that some undetermined amount of cheating took place. It was widely assumed that a large number of "mom and pop" stores succumbed to pressure from long-time customers to give them cash for their blue coupons or to let them use those coupons for food not on the USDA list.

Congress had been only peripherally involved with the first food stamp plan. After administrators ended the program, a few congressmen, especially Senator George Aiken (R.–Vt.), pushed for a specific authorization for food stamps to supplement the discretionary authority already available to the secretary of agriculture. During the 1940s, Aiken received only nominal support from Secretaries of Agriculture

Clinton Anderson and Charles Brannan. As a result, his bills made little headway in the Congress. When the Republicans came into power in 1952, President Dwight Eisenhower appointed a staunch conservative, Ezra Taft Benson, to head USDA. Benson was not sympathetic to food stamps, and prospects for a new program did not appear to be bright for the remainder of the Eisenhower administration.

The idea of a food stamp program was nevertheless kept alive in both the Department of Agriculture and the Congress. The individuals who administered the first food stamp plan were still employed in the department. Despite the lack of support from the secretary's office, they continued to believe that the program was a viable one. "Whenever we talked about surpluses, we talked about food stamps," recalled one former official. On the congressional side, Aiken was joined in the cause by Representative Leonor Sullivan (D.–Mo.), who was elected to her late husband's seat in 1952. Congresswoman Sullivan, a tenacious and determined legislator, became the most important congressional advocate of a food stamp program. During the 1950s she made slow but steady progress in moving the Congress toward adoption of a food stamp plan.

Mrs. Sullivan believed that the commodity distribution program, which had been reinstituted by USDA, was an ineffective means of reaching the poor. Although not a member of the House Agriculture Committee, she was able to work with its chairman, Harold Cooley (D.–N.C.). By 1956 she succeeded in persuading Congress to request a food stamp feasibility study from USDA. Unsurprisingly, the report sent by Benson and his aides was not enthusiastic.[4] In 1957 and 1958 food stamp proposals were defeated on the floor of the House. Undaunted, Congresswoman Sullivan stubbornly pursued her goal. She became a thorn in the side of the Democratic leadership, using whatever tactics she could to press for a food stamp program. She objected to unanimous consent agreements on the floor until "[Speaker] Rayburn asked me what I wanted and I told him."

By 1959 the party leadership was willing to go along with Congresswoman Sullivan. When the House Rules Committee refused to send a food stamp bill to the floor, the leadership quietly supported her effort to bring the bill to a vote. When the vote was taken, a food stamp proposal passed for the first time. The price for passage was high: The bill (an amendment to another agriculture bill) did not make the program mandatory.[5] Since nothing had changed Secretary Benson's mind, he exercised his option to do nothing. Mrs. Sullivan never forgave him. She did not understand why USDA did not have more compassion for the needy she had seen in the slums of St. Louis. "We seem to be able to send chickens to Egypt, but we can't provide them to our poorest here," she told her House colleagues.[6] But feeding the hungry was only an incidental activity of USDA in the 1950s. An adequate diet for every American had yet to become a right. Whatever its obligation, USDA felt that it was doing its part through the commodity distribution program.

FOOD STAMPS RETURN

USDA's self-satisfaction notwithstanding, the commodity program was an abysmal failure. Those in Congress and in the department who argued that the commodity program was effectively combatting hunger were taking part in a cruel hoax. Degrading and poorly administered, the program was available only in certain areas of the country. In 1959 eleven states did not participate in the commodity program, and seven others served less than 10 percent of their citizens on public assistance.[7] In counties that did participate, individuals had to line up at the welfare office or elsewhere to receive a package of food that was hardly appealing. Excessive quantities of certain items would be included each month. Simply speaking, a family could eat only so much cheese. A common complaint was that local welfare administrators did not really care about the program and that their eligibility requirements were too lax or arbitrary. But the biggest problem with the commodity program was that it just did not provide enough food. In 1960, the last year of the Eisenhower administration, the commodity program offered recipients a monthly package worth only $2.20 and containing just five items: lard, rice, flour, butter, and cheese.

The malnutrition and hunger that existed in spite of the commodity program was evident to John F. Kennedy as he campaigned in the presidential primaries. Kennedy was particularly moved by the unconscionable destitution he observed in West Virginia, a state that had one of the most extensive commodity programs. He also spoke about hunger during the general election campaign against Richard Nixon. During their first televised debate, Kennedy cited the hunger problem in a dynamic opening statement. He told the 65 million viewers that he had seen children in West Virginia taking part of their school lunches home with them. Kennedy ridiculed the commodity program and forcefully declared that government was not doing enough to feed the poor.

Kennedy did not forget what he had seen during the campaign. His first executive order, issued on the day after his inauguration, instructed the secretary of agriculture "to expand and improve" the commodity distribution program. Increasing the number of food products in the commodity packages was something the president could do immediately, but he did not consider that a long-term solution. Indeed, Kennedy had previously introduced a food stamp bill in the Senate. Nor were the liberals in Congress going to allow him to forget. Leonor Sullivan had been in touch with Kennedy during the transition. "On the day he was inaugurated, there was a memo on his desk reminding him that he promised a food stamp program," she reminisced proudly.

USDA wasted no time: A food stamp task force was set up even before Kennedy took office. The small working group included Howard P. Davis, Sam Vanneman, and Isabelle Kelley. Davis and Vanneman had been involved with the first food stamp program. Kelley had come to the department during World War II from graduate study in agricultural economics at Iowa State University. Davis, Vanneman, and Kelley would become the program's most important administrators in the decade to come.

The working group was convinced that the two-color system of the first food stamp plan was awkward and unnecessary. "The increase in consumption was in spite of the two-color system," said one task force member. Nor were these early planners in favor of Congresswoman Sullivan's bill, which designated all stamps for surplus goods only. Instead, they thought the best way to run the program would be to approximate the free market by letting people buy whatever they wanted with their stamps. The increased buying power would result in an expansion of demand that could not help but reduce surplus commodities. The remaining questions before the task force were not so easily resolved. How many stamps should recipients get, and how much should they be charged for them?

On February 2, 1961, Kennedy sent a message to Capitol Hill stating that, under the authority granted to him by Congress (Mrs. Sullivan's 1959 amendment), he was directing Secretary of Agriculture Orville Freeman "to proceed as rapidly as possible" with the establishment of food stamp pilot projects. When Kennedy's formal directive reached USDA a few weeks later, a second task force was set up to

make the final decisions on the nature of the food stamp program. Again, Howard Davis (head of the Food Distribution Division of the Agricultural Marketing Service), Sam Vanneman, and Isabelle Kelley emerged as the key figures on the committee. Davis, who would have formal authority over the pilot projects, was, in the words of one USDA official, "the ultimate bureaucrat." He was cautious, loyal to his superiors, and considered to be an effective administrator. This second task force had to work quickly. "Freeman let us know that he damn well wanted the pilot projects in operation by June," said one member. In addition to formulating the price and allocation formulas, the task force had to write all other guidelines and regulations, select the project areas, and develop contractual and working relationships with the local authorities who would administer the program.

The job of deciding how many coupons to give and how much to charge for them fell to Isabelle Kelley and Sam Vanneman. Some thought had been given by the first task force to allotting each family the amount of coupons equivalent to USDA's economy food plan. The economy food plan was the lowest cost, nutritionally adequate diet that had been developed by USDA home economists. In 1961 it corresponded to about five dollars worth of food per person per week.[8] In contemplating their decision, Kelley and Vanneman looked at statistics on home expenditures from the Bureau of Agricultural Economics. When expenditures were plotted against income, food purchasing could be seen to rise with income. Because of these figures, Kelley felt that it would be bad planning to give all families the full number of coupons commensurate with the economy food plan—that is, the eighty dollars worth of coupons necessary for a diet equivalent to that of the economy food plan for a family of four at the bottom end of the income scale. If the amount of stamps was too far in excess of what the family normally spent on food, there would be a great temptation for them to try to sell some of the stamps for cash on a newly created black market.

The fear of scandal was an important factor in the task force's thinking. If a significant number of food stamps were traded illegally, the program's very existence could be jeopardized. The members of the working group were mindful of the allegations of cheating and fraud that had been made about the first food stamp program. With fragile support in the Congress, it was essential that this type of problem be avoided as much as possible. To combat this possibility, Kelley and Vanneman set up allocation tables that used a sliding scale. As a fami-

26

ly's income rose, so did its coupon allotment (see Table 1). Recipients at the lower end of the income scale would not receive enough stamps to purchase a diet at the level of the economy food plan, thus breaking any link between the program and a nutritional standard. Coupon allotments would provide more food, but not necessarily enough for a decent, nutritious diet.

The purchase price for food stamps was also graduated on a sliding scale. Davis, Kelley, and Vanneman felt strongly that recipients should buy their stamps for an amount roughly equal to what they usually spent on food. In return for their cash payment, participants would receive stamps of an equal dollar amount, plus some free "bonus" stamps. If families were simply given their bonus stamps without having to pay anything, there was no assurance that they would increase their overall food purchasing. Setting the purchase price on a scale adjustable to what a family generally spent on food would mini-

Table 1. Initial Food Stamp Plan, Kentucky and Pennsylvania, 1961

Monthly income	Purchase requirement		Value of bonus stamps		Total value of stamps	
(four-person families)	Ky.	Pa.	Ky.	Pa.	Ky.	Pa.
$ 0–24	$ 0	$ 0	$40	$46	$40	$46
25–34	18	0	42	46	60	46
35–44	28	10	40	44	68	54
45–54	32	16	38	42	70	58
55–64	36	22	36	40	72	62
65–74	40	28	34	38	74	66
75–84	44	34	32	36	76	70
85–94	48	40	30	34	78	74
95–104	52	44	28	34	80	78
105–114	56	48	26	32	82	80
115–124	60	50	24	32	84	82
125–134[a]	64	54	24	30	88	84
135–144		56		30		86
145–154		60		28		88
155–174		64		26		90
175–194		68		24		92
195–209		72		22		94
210–245[b]		76		20		96

[a]Four-person families with income above this interval were not eligible in Kentucky
[b]Four-person families with income above this interval were not eligible in Pennsylvania

SOURCE: USDA, History Group Files.

mize the substitution of coupons for dollars normally spent on food. By charging families for their coupon allotment, the program would make it certain that participants expanded their demand for food and helped the farmers as well as themselves.

Eligibility for the food stamp program was based on the income cut-off line used in each state for public assistance. Individuals or families did not have to be otherwise eligible for welfare to qualify for food stamps. Thus, persons who did not fall into one of the categories usually associated with various welfare programs, such as blindness, disability, or fatherless families, could qualify for food stamps. They only had to be poor.

By the middle of May 1961 the administrative guidelines were largely finished. The regulations that appeared in the *Federal Register* about this time were rather sparse, taking up only about three pages. The published regulations dealt mostly with the certification of households and the mechanics of coupon redemption. The most important guidelines, the purchase price and the allotment tables, were not published in the *Federal Register*.[9] The decisions by Davis, Kelley, and Vanneman were largely autonomous, with little input from the secretary's office or from the Congress. There was almost no public discussion of what the program should look like. At the time, the details of the new program seemed to be technical matters, not substantive policy.

MAKING THE PROGRAM WORK

The first of eight food stamp pilot projects started up in McDowell County, West Virginia, on May 29, 1961.[10] Secretary Freeman went to Welch, West Virginia, to present the first stamps to Alderson Muncy, an unemployed miner, his wife, and their thirteen children. Tom Wicker told readers of the *New York Times* that Muncy's first purchase at Henderson's supermarket was a "huge can of pork and beans."[11] Soon all the projects were in operation, and the immediate reaction in the media was generally favorable. Typical was the *Pittsburgh Press's* description of the nearby Fayette County project as a "success." It quoted one state official as saying, "Deliveries of fresh milk are way up, meat sales have increased and canned goods are being bought by the case again." The same official concluded, "I've seen gratitude in the eyes and voices of these people. It makes my job worthwhile."[12]

A SECOND CHANCE FOR FOOD STAMPS

The pilot projects were studied closely by social scientists from USDA's Economic Research Service. The program administrators' primary concern was the impact of the program on retail sales of food and on individual food consumption. In both areas they had reason to be pleased. Grocery stores in project areas experienced a significant increase in sales, and the diets of participants were shown to have improved also. At the end of 1961 Isabelle Kelley began to put together a summary report for USDA on the first half-year of the program. Citing the statistics on food sales and family diet, as well as the strong administrative performance, she concluded that the program was achieving its goals. She recommended that the program be gradually expanded.[13]

However, one disturbing trend did emerge from the early evaluation research. As counties switched from commodity distribution to food stamps, participation dropped precipitously. In May 1961 approximately 310,000 persons were receiving commodity packages in the eight pilot project areas. In November, five months after the switch to food stamps had been completed, there were only around 138,000 participants. Nevertheless, Kelley's summary evaluation did not view these figures with alarm. A lower participation rate for the food stamp program was to be expected, she noted, because many low-income families could purchase good diets even with their limited funds. The price structure was also acknowledged as a contributing factor to the lower level of participation. Yet it was deemed understandable that individuals at the upper end of the income scale, who had to pay more for their stamps, would feel that they did not get enough in return for their purchase price to make it worth their while to participate.[14]

In light of the first year's experience, decisions had to be made as to whether any changes in the program were needed. The White House was happy with the program and the favorable press it had received. Its only real preference was that the program be expanded. Orville Freeman, preoccupied with other matters, was satisfied as well. Davis and his colleagues continued with few constraints on their authority over the program.

As reflected in Kelley's summary report, there was little feeling at the operational and administrative levels that major reforms were needed. The most important decision about program reform was really a nondecision. Since USDA officials did not view the lower participation rate as a problem, no changes were made to stimulate greater participation. A few minor adjustments lowered the cost of stamps to some, but the price of stamps was actually raised for others at the bottom end of the income scale. The reason given for raising the purchase price was that recipients in some project areas were receiving their stamps for free. In Fayette County, Pennsylvania, for example, all participants with a family income of less than $35 a month paid nothing for their stamps. Howard Davis had never liked the idea of free stamps, and Kelley and Vanneman began to feel the same way. At the bottom income rung the price for food stamps was reset at two dollars a person.

The abolition of free stamps for the most impoverished participants reflected the personal philosophies of the early administrators. The three key administrators believed that the price for stamps should be based on an individual's "normal" expenditures for food. Although it was true that some individuals might have no income for a month, they still had to spend money on food somehow, whether they borrowed it or were forced to seek some cash assistance from the government. It was the administrators' strong conviction that the essence of the program was self-help. Individuals would spend their normal amount on food and would receive free bonus stamps in return. To achieve true demand increase, rather than a simple substitution of stamps for dollars that would be spent at the grocery store anyway, there had to be a purchase price for all recipients.

The theoretical foundation of the program had come to rest on this "normal expenditure" concept. The purchase price would continue to be related to what research showed to be the average amount of food purchases by families at various income levels. If anything, the two-dollar price for those at the bottom was generous—no one really lived on that little. "There was no survey that showed people spending only $2.00 a month on food," stated one of the administrators. But two dollars was at least politically acceptable, and the normal concept was preserved. *Food stamps was to be a self-help program, and everyone would pay something for the stamps.*

The administrative guidelines, as constructed by Davis, Vanneman, and Kelley, had designed the program. With the few modifications made after the review of the first pilot projects, the basic structure of the program was fixed for the rest of the decade. The success of the pilot projects led President Kennedy to announce in August 1962 that twenty-five new projects would be initiated. By December there were plans for forty more.

The second round of food stamp projects produced the first real criticism of the program. Two very large urban areas, St. Louis and Cleveland, were among the new project areas, and in both cities the food stamp program was an immediate failure. Administrators could not rationalize away an extremely low participation rate as expected or understandable. The disastrous performance in St. Louis was acutely embarrassing, for it was the home district of Leonor Sullivan.

Although Detroit, the only large city among the first eight projects, had lost 110,000 individuals when it switched from commodities to food stamps, it was St. Louis and Cleveland that forced the issue.[15] Congresswoman Sullivan would later testify at a committee hearing that only 1,000 of the estimated 50,000 participants in the commodity program in St. Louis took part in the food stamp program during its first month.[16] When it became clear that the food stamp program was failing in St. Louis, Mrs. Sullivan voiced her concerns to Secretary Freeman. Freeman did not have to prompt Davis or his aides. They were already alarmed over the situation in St. Louis and Cleveland. At the same time, however, they stubbornly refused to believe that the basic structure of the program was unsound. They continued to feel that lack of participation was largely a reflection of rational economic behavior: Individuals weigh the costs and benefits of potential actions and then act accordingly. As one of the early administrators argued many years later, "The basic thing was that in spite of all the things you heard about hunger, these families didn't feel the need for more food. They felt the need for more money. If they could get by without the stamps before the program, then they could get by without the program and without paying out their money." The program administrators could not accept that the pricing system for the stamps made the cost of participation artificially high and unduly discouraged enrollment in the program. Still, Davis, Vanneman, and Kelley were not politically naive, and they knew that changes had to be made.

To determine what changes should be made, Davis and Kelley decided to go to Cleveland to inspect the program there. Before they left, the two met with Leonor Sullivan and agreed to visit St. Louis as well. To the welfare workers in Cleveland and St. Louis, the problem with the program could not be more obvious. They showed Davis and Kelley numerous cases where a family's rent and food stamp purchase price exceeded its monthly income from welfare. It was not a matter of economic rationality; rather, for many the grants from the AFDC program were not large enough. At the base of the problem, of course, was the refusal of Ohio and Missouri to give their citizens on welfare enough to live on. Davis and Kelley did not have the option of re-forming state-run AFDC programs. The changes would have to be made in the food stamp program.

The common denominator between St. Louis and Cleveland was the high cost of housing. A means had to be devised to compensate for the higher living costs of those who resided in northern, urban areas as opposed to the less expensive mining regions of Kentucky or Pennsylvania. The solution was a hardship shelter deduction. Each family's rent (or mortgage), electricity, and heat bills would be added up by food stamp certification workers during the application process. If the amount was excessive, the family could be compensated by a shelter deduction. Isabelle Kelley and Grant Tolley, another administrator in the Food Distribution Division, examined cost-of-living figures to determine what the formula should be. Thirty percent of a family's income seemed to be the average cost for shelter expense, and this became the standard. All shelter expenses above 30 percent were deducted from a family's income before their purchase price for food stamps was figured. The higher a family's shelter costs (above the 30 percent threshold), the lower their food stamps purchase price.[17]

In addition to the shelter deduction, a few other deductions were formalized as well. In the first round of pilot projects administrators had allowed local case workers to deduct unusually high medical costs or emergency expenses—a funeral, for example—from a family's gross income. After these deductions were defined and openly approved by Washington, pressure grew from local welfare administrators for a child care deduction for working mothers. This logical work incentive was approved as well.[18] The deductions instituted around this time signified an important change in the way the food stamp purchase price was calculated. For the purposes of the food stamp program, a family's income was coming to mean *disposable* income after certain necessary expenses were paid.

The shelter deduction was a meaningful way of reducing the cost of stamps for urban dwellers. Equally significantly, it allowed administrators to sidestep the issue of whether or not the purchase price should be abolished or openly cut across the board. The crisis had been forestalled. Participation picked up a little, and soon complacency about the program would set in. Four years later, in 1967, Leonor Sullivan would say proudly of the St. Louis program, "We had the regulations made more flexible and now we have three times as many people participating as we did at first."[19] She, along with the program administrators, did not seem concerned that participation was still less than half of what it had been in the St. Louis commodity distribution program.

A PROGRAM BECOMES A BILL, A BILL BECOMES A LAW

With both the White House and Secretary Freeman satisfied that the pilot projects were a success, a decision was made to request congressional approval of an ongoing food stamp program. In January 1963, with the second round of projects just starting up, President Kennedy asked for funding for the program in his budget message to Congress. If the program were to continue to expand, it needed a specific authorization and appropriation.

The food stamp plan appeared to have a decent chance of passage. Although the public was not intensely interested in the program, the stories in the press had helped to create a positive image for food stamps. The Senate appeared to be favorably inclined, and it seemed possible that a majority could be produced in the House. The biggest problem was with the House Committee on Agriculture. Although Chairman Harold Cooley stood behind the plan, the balance of power within the committee was in the hands of a coalition of Republicans and southern Democrats. By themselves, they would have killed the program. Nevertheless, the skill and fortitude of Leonor Sullivan, together with the help of the House leadership, overcame the resistance of the committee. In a committee-based policy-making body like the House, it is unusual for leadership on an issue to fall to someone outside of the committee. Mrs. Sullivan's leadership is a tribute to her dedication, but it is also a stark indication of the lack of interest in food stamps within the Agriculture Committee.

The food stamp bill, drafted in USDA under the careful eye of Howard Davis, was the subject of committee hearings in June 1963. The department was already envisioning a large-scale program, with costs rising to $360 million annually within five years. The House Agriculture Committee had to be pushed hard to move at all on the bill. "Freeman went to Congress with his beautiful program and found that nobody cared," said one USDA official in retrospect. The department tried to modify the legislation in order to make it more politically acceptable, but in early February 1964 the committee tabled the bill.

33

Immediately, though, there was talk of food stamp advocates attempting to revive the bill by taking action against another agriculture bill in the hope of generating a logroll.[20]

Knowing that the administration wanted the food stamp plan, and realizing that Mrs. Sullivan would do what she could to hold up other agricultural legislation, the House leadership acted quickly to resuscitate the bill. It retaliated against the Southerners on the Agriculture Committee by having a bill sponsoring tobacco research held up in the Rules Committee. When it became apparent that the tobacco bill was being held hostage, three Democrats on the Agriculture Committee switched their votes on the food stamp bill. A little over a month after the Rules Committee action, the food stamp bill was voted out of the Agriculture Committee by a two-vote margin. No committee Republicans voted for the bill.[21]

Gathering a majority for the bill on the floor of the House also proved to be a struggle. For months key congressional and USDA staffers—including Davis, Vanneman, Kelley, House Agricultural Committee counsel John Heimburger, Sullivan staffer Charles Holstein, and Freeman legislative aide Ken Birkhead—worked hard to make the bill agreeable to potential supporters. As Randall Ripley has vividly demonstrated, final passage of the food stamp plan involved a classic case of legislative logrolling.[22] Two pieces of legislation, the food stamp proposal and a cotton-wheat subsidy bill, apparently lacked majorities in the House. As it became evident that both bills were in trouble, northern Democrats who wanted food stamps (but not cotton-wheat) and southern Democrats and a few Republicans who wanted cotton-wheat (but not food stamps) became logical partners for a trade-off.[23] Ripley describes the trade as the product of a "favorable psychological climate." It was not even necessary to have a formal meeting for bargaining purposes—the talk and press commentary convinced everyone that the logroll would take place.[24] This does not mean that no solicitation of votes occurred. As one Democratic member of the Agriculture Committee put it, "You never use the word 'deal.' But Mrs. Sullivan talked to Cooley, she talked to me, and it was pretty well understood that there would be this type of help."

In the end the deal held, and both bills passed—food stamps by 229–189, cotton-wheat by a much narrower 211–203. The Senate soon responded, and the bill became law on August 31, 1964.[25] In signing the legislation, President Lyndon Johnson told those present that the "Food Stamp Act weds the best of the humanitarian instincts of the

American people with the best of the free enterprise system."[26] He also paid special tribute to Representative Leonor Sullivan and Senator George Aiken. They had finally prevailed.

The basic issue in the congressional debate over food stamps was really the ideological division that has traditionally divided conservatives and liberals: To what degree is the federal government responsible for taking care of the poor? To most conservatives, including almost all Republicans, the food stamp plan was just one more expensive raid on the Treasury, one more instance of excessive federal growth. Still, there were enough liberals, moderates, and cotton-wheat vote traders to get the bill through the House. In the last analysis, though, its passage was the result of legislative maneuvering, not policy consensus.

STABILITY AND SUCCESS

The passage of the Food Stamp Act of 1964 actually had little impact on program operations. The new law did permit substantial expansion of the program, but the Food Distribution Division policies already in operation were little changed. The Food Stamp Act of 1964 did not create basic food stamp policy. Rather, it legitimated and ratified the administrative guidelines already in effect.

As they made the key decisions in the first few years of the pilot projects, Davis, Vanneman, and Kelley surely anticipated congressional sentiment. They carefully avoided doing anything that might cause undue antagonism in the Congress. Nevertheless, they enjoyed great latitude in making critical decisions. There was no obvious congressional preference on many of the issues they faced. Nor was there any great congressional interest. Only Leonor Sullivan kept an eye on program implementation and even her influence was hardly impressive. Davis, Vanneman, and Kelley had, after all, rejected the food stamp plan that had been passed at her initiative in 1959. Instead, they designed a program of their own liking.

Davis and his two chief subordinates had influenced the outcome in the House by their care in wording the legislation and by their efforts to keep unwanted amendments out of the bill. In the years immediately following passage of the Food Stamp Act, their authority over the program continued unchecked. The Agriculture Committees of the

Congress remained uninterested in the program. For her part, Congresswoman Sullivan felt that USDA was doing a good job of administering food stamps.

All the important administrative guidelines developed before and during the pilot projects changed little in the next few years. The underlying philosophy of the program's pricing structure had been written into the law. The statute required that recipients be charged their "normal expenditures" for food when they received their stamps. The decision of program officials not to offer participants the amount of stamps equal to a nutritionally adequate diet was also endorsed by the new law. The coupon allotments would only provide recipients "with an opportunity to obtain a more nutritionally adequate diet." Since the law mostly restated what had been decided prior to its passage, few significant regulations or guidelines were generated in its wake.

The internal administration of the food stamp program remained generally stable. There was a reorganization in 1965, when the Agricultural Marketing Service, which had line authority over food stamps, became the Consumer and Marketing Service. The subordinate Food Distribution Division was absorbed into Consumer Food Programs. Howard Davis retained overall responsibility for food stamps as deputy administrator for Consumer Food Programs. Sam Vanneman remained as an aide to Davis, and Isabelle Kelley headed the Food Stamp Division within Consumer Food Programs. In terms of the day-to-day operation of the program, Kelley was becoming increasingly important. An intelligent, genial woman, she was widely respected by those working with her.

Whatever the formal lines of authority, Davis continued to be directly responsible to Orville Freeman. The White House's role was minimal, and it gave little direction to the department. With Johnson's re-election in 1964, attention turned to the social programs proposed as part of the new War on Poverty. Since the food stamp program appeared to have no major problems, Davis and his aides were left pretty much alone.

The period between late 1964 and early 1967 was one of quiet growth for the program. In describing this era, one USDA official said, "There really wasn't much in the way of policy questions then. . . . The important decisions were deciding which counties would get the program." Indeed, the program was quite in demand, as congressmen wanted to reap the good will and publicity that accompanied the opening of a new project. At this time there was always a long waiting list of counties that wanted to join the program. Only funding controlled the growth of the program as it expanded from 43 projects in 1964 to 324 in 1966.

The food stamp program seemed to be an unqualified success. The participation rate had ceased to be an issue. The public and the press remained strongly supportive. Who could argue with this humane approach to feeding hungry Americans? Even the conservative *Wall Street Journal* praised the program. In a September 1966 article it described how "a school teacher recently told welfare officials of the reaction when she called in a parent to exclaim on the remarkable improvement in her child's work. "The mother broke into tears and said that for the first time in his life the child was getting enough to eat under the food stamp program.' "[27] Few doubted that the food stamp program was winning the battle against hunger.

HOW REGULATIONS ARE WRITTEN: ADMINISTRATIVE AUTONOMY

The most striking aspect of food stamp policy making during these early years is the independence of the administrators. Davis, Kelley, and Vanneman had the luxury of being able to design and administer the program with little outside interference. They were competent, hard-working bureaucrats, and they surely merited confidence in their abilities. Nonetheless, it might seem surprising that they operated with such little direction from the Congress and from administration superiors.

It is clear that the autonomy enjoyed by Davis and his colleagues was enhanced by the unusual nature of the issue. As a plan intended to alleviate farm surpluses as well as hunger, the food stamp idea was first regarded as a policy requiring the expertise of agriculture specialists. Consequently, the program came under the authority of congressional committees and a cabinet department that cared little about it. Members of the Agriculture Committees, disproportionately from farm states, were primarily concerned with price supports for commodities grown by their constituents.[28] Most members perceived food stamps as an issue that was relatively unimportant to the voters back home. Similarly, the top officials in USDA considered their primary constituents to be farmers; the clientele for food stamps was of peripheral interest to them.

Although the conception of food stamps as a farm issue may have contributed to the independence of administrators, that perspective still does not entirely explain the behavior of administrators. Given the tenuous support for the program in Congress, why did administrators choose such an independent path? Political scientists have long held that it is rational for administrators to expend considerable resources to build up maximum support for their programs in the Congress. Moreover, the relationship between Congress and administrative agencies is often criticized for being too close. Informal bargaining is generally seen as mutually rewarding. Why, then, was there little consultation with Congress in the development of food stamp program policy? Although some members of the Agriculture Committees were unwaveringly opposed to food stamps, others were at least sympathetic. Even Leonor Sullivan, food stamp's most vital sponsor, was ignored when the basic design of the program was being determined. Sullivan's own food stamp plan was quickly discarded by the three key administrators.

Despite the program's vulnerable position, its administrators did not view a close working relationship with the Congress as desirable. On the contrary, Davis and the others preferred to avoid consultation if at all possible. Program support in the Congress was a secondary goal. *The most important objective of the program administrators was to retain and maximize their autonomy.* For that reason, administrators deemed it wise to eschew a consultative relationship with Congress.

Although the administrators successfully maintained their independence, they were acutely aware of problems that could emerge with the Congress. Davis, Kelley, and Vanneman made firm judgments as to the types of policies that could lead to trouble with the House or Senate. Uppermost in their minds was the fear of congressional reaction to reports of widespread cheating in the program. As a result, the income and coupon tables were constructed to diminish the chance that coupons could be black-marketed. Yet even this decision was in line with the administrators' own thinking and was not made merely in deference to the Congress.

In sum, the administrators made decisions concerning program guidelines within a range of options they considered acceptable to the Congress. The House and the Senate were viewed as potentially meddlesome, while basic program design was seen as the proper responsibility of administrators. Autonomy was to be protected, so little was done to nurture a cooperative relationship with the Congress.

A SECOND CHANCE FOR FOOD STAMPS

As will be shown in the remainder of this narrative, administrators were not always able to operate with such independence. As the program became more controversial and the Congress became more aggressive, administrators had to alter their patterns of decision making. In the concluding chapter of this study, administrative autonomy and discretionary authority will be examined further. An attempt will be made to come to an understanding of the trade-off between the desire for autonomy and the need for congressional cooperation.

2
HUNGER BECOMES
AN ISSUE

THE CIVIL RIGHTS AND Vietnam antiwar movements marked the 1960s as a decade of protest, activism, and widespread dissatisfaction with government. At the same time, the social programs of Lyndon Johnson's Great Society led to rising expectations on the part of the poor. Surely those who championed these social programs harbored unrealistic expectations of what the Great Society could accomplish in a relatively short time.[1] Critics charged that the Johnson and Nixon administrations were not doing nearly enough to solve the problems of the underprivileged. Concurrently, government was being pushed in the opposite direction by angry citizens who felt that many new government programs unduly favored minorities at the expense of the white middle class.

The food stamp program would not remain unscathed by these years of social protest. Demands mounted from food stamp supporters for a more effective and generous program. Reform was never easy, however, and policy changes were slow to come.

THE MISSING PARTICIPANTS

The problem of low participation, first evidenced in the pilot projects, continued to plague the program as it expanded into new areas of the country. In general, after a county switched from commodities to food stamps, overall participation dropped considerably. The experience gained during the program's first five years of operation provided few answers toward solving the problem. Even in the late 1960s, new project openings were almost inevitably accompanied by a sizable drop in the participation levels that had been established under the commodity distribution program. Howard Davis, Isabelle Kelley, and the others remained convinced that there were two justifiable reasons for the lower participation rate. First, eligibility under the commodity distribution program was notoriously lax. Many local welfare administrators did not really care who got the food; they just wanted to get rid of it. Some commodity recipients were not applying for food stamps because they knew that they would not qualify under the more rigorous eligibility standards. Second, administrators continued to argue that a large number of the eligible individuals who did not participate were rational actors at the top of the sliding income scale. These people had to pay out a lot of cash for a small bonus; it would be reasonable to expect them to participate at a lower rate.

Yet the extent of the participation decline convinced some critics that many of the missing participants fell into neither the ineligible nor the rational actor category. Enrollment figures through January 1, 1969, showed that participation in food stamp programs in most states was 30 to 60 percent lower than that in the earlier commodity programs. In Illinois, for example, some 68,000 individuals were "missing" from the food stamp program—a 61 percent drop. Pennsylvania's showing of only a 46 percent decline still meant that close to 200,000 commodity recipients had failed to sign up for food stamps.[2]

When the Agriculture Department was questioned as to why the participation rate dropped so low when counties switched to food stamps, it often replied with an expression of reassurance that participation would climb to a respectable figure after people had had a chance to learn about the program. Yet participation never increased significantly. After a couple of years in the program, a project area's rate was likely to be only 40 to 60 percent of what it had been under commodities.[3] Moreover, some drops were so disastrous that no rationalization offered by USDA made any sense. East Carrol Parish, Louisiana, went in one month from 5,180 commodity recipients to 728 food stamp recipients. Participation did improve some, but it was still less than 2,000 individuals after the first three months. In Chicot County, Arkansas, participation actually declined over time, a phenomenon precisely opposite from the department's predictions. In the first month the drop was only from 5,791 to 4,965 recipients. But participation dropped sharply in the next four months to 2,628, until it began it climb a little. Obviously, many individuals in Chicot County tried the program and then decided against it.[4]

USDA simply would not admit that a serious participation problem existed. And Congress largely remained an uncritical partner until the end of the Johnson administration. As Gilbert Steiner notes, "Through the seven years beginning in 1961, the congressional and administrative groups struck a tolerable balance. Either not knowing better or not wishing to disturb that balance, they all gave assurances that everything was just right with food stamps."[5] Leonor Sullivan, still the recognized leader on food stamp policy in Congress, continued to believe that the shelter deduction had solved the participation problem.

The belief of Davis, Kelley, and other officials that nothing was fundamentally wrong with the program was reinforced by their own research. The terrible participation problem that became apparent in the Cleveland and St. Louis pilot projects provoked the administrators to undertake an in-depth study of participation. St. Louis was chosen as the test site, and in May and June of 1964 USDA conducted a survey of eligible nonparticipants. Although 38 percent of the respondents cited the purchase price or the lack of income as their reason for not participating, the report concluded that the purchase price was "reasonable." The survey found that 85 percent of the nonparticipants were spending more cash for food in a month than they would have paid for stamps. It made no sense for the nonparticipants to continue abstaining from the program. Robert Reese and Sadye Adelson, the two USDA economists who wrote the report, concluded that only marginal changes in the purchase price were needed.[6] It would take some time before the administrators and staffers in USDA would begin to understand the economics of being poor.

PEOPLE ARE STARVING

It is difficult to explain how societal problems become political issues. Each issue has a unique mixture of factors that force it into the national limelight. Sometimes issues arise out of a clearly defined crisis, such as the Arab oil embargo of 1973. The origins of other issues are not so clear. When, for example, did the so-called "welfare mess" begin?[7]

Hunger was not an issue of any consequence in 1966. What, then, explains its development as a political issue in 1967? Although some events that occurred in 1967 and afterwards can be cited as catalysts behind the hunger issue, its origins can be traced back a little further—to the civil rights movement, to the increasing social concern and activism that came out of the Kennedy years, and to the awareness of deprivation in America that was fostered by Johnson's War on Poverty proposals. For these and other reasons, the hunger problem captured the imagination of a number of politicians, journalists, lawyers, and social activists. These individuals found hunger to be a compelling problem that suited their ideological attitudes and personal ambitions.

Although the statistics showed that the food stamp program was failing to reach large numbers of potential recipients, it was not the figures on food stamp participation that brought the hunger issue into the national spotlight. The enrollment figures for various states and counties were only of secondary importance in the development of national recognition of the hunger problem. Rather, it was the personal portraits of individual suffering and malnutrition, conveyed through the media, that made some Americans realize that other Americans were going hungry.

"The big change came when Bobby Kennedy got into the act," said one Agriculture official. Kennedy participated in hearings of the Subcommittee on Employment, Manpower, and Poverty of the Senate Labor and Public Welfare Committee. Together with subcommittee chairman Joseph Clark (D.–Pa.), Jacob Javits (R.–N.Y.), and George Murphy (R.–Calif.), he went to Mississippi in April 1967 to examine the effectiveness of poverty programs. At hearings held in Jackson, many of the poor themselves testified before the subcommittee. The situation in Mississippi was succinctly described by a young N A A C P lawyer, Marian Wright, who bluntly told the subcommittee, "People are starving."[8]

The following day Kennedy and Clark visited some rural areas of the Mississippi Delta. In small towns like Greenville they saw not only shanties and squalor but listless babies and demoralized adults as well. Hunger was a stark reality evident all over the Delta. Kennedy's and Clark's trip, which had been intended to attract press coverage of the issue, received a modest amount of publicity. The *New York Times* reported the story on page 29, *Time* gave it two paragraphs, and *Newsweek* ignored it altogether.[9] Kennedy was no ordinary politician, of course, and the trip took on a great deal of symbolic value. To the poor he represented the hope that something would be done. In Washington he was someone who could effectively plead the case for assistance before USDA. When they returned to Washington, Kennedy and Clark went to see Orville Freeman. They also began plans for more subcommittee hearings. The issue had finally begun to surface.

The trip to Mississippi and the ensuing criticism of the administration by members of the subcommittee stimulated activity on other fronts. The Field Foundation, a liberal philanthropic institution, took notice of the subcommittee's trip to Mississippi. The director of the foundation, Leslie Dunbar, had participated in antipoverty drives in the South and was sympathetic to Kennedy's and Clark's efforts. Dunbar phoned Harvard University psychiatrist Robert Coles and asked him to go to Mississippi with a team of doctors to gather medical evidence on malnutrition.[10] Coles, who had done extensive research on the effects of poverty on children, accepted Dunbar's offer, and a team of doctors left for Mississippi the following month. The Coles group traveled throughout the Delta, paying special attention to the physical conditions of the children of this predominantly black area. After writing up their report, they testified before the Clark subcommittee in July. Their report is a chilling account of abject poverty and malnutrition:

> We saw children afflicted with chronic diarrhea, chronic sores, chronic leg and arm (untreated) injuries and deformities. We saw homes without running water, without electricity, without screens, in which children drink contaminated water and live with germ-bearing mosquitoes and flies everywhere around. We saw homes with children who are lucky to eat one meal a day—and that one inadequate so far as vitamins, minerals, or protein is concerned. We saw children who don't get to drink milk, don't get to eat fruit, green vegetables, or meat. They live on starches—grits, bread, Kool-Aid. Their parents may be declared ineligible for commodities, ineligible for the food stamp program, even though they have literally nothing. We saw children fed communally—that is by neighbors who give scraps of food to children whose own parents have nothing to give them. Not only are these children receiving no food from the government, they are also getting no medical attention whatsoever. They are out of sight and ignored. They are living under such primitive conditions that we found it hard to believe we were examining American children of the twentieth century.[11]

HUNGER BECOMES AN ISSUE

The medical data gathered by these doctors played an important role in fostering public awareness of the hunger problem. The Coles group was so clear in its findings and so strong in its presentation that the charges of widespread hunger were now incontrovertible. That the authors of the report were physicians gave their criticisms added legitimacy. Skeptics could no longer dismiss what Kennedy and Clark had "discovered" as political grandstanding.

The doctors' testimony before the Clark subcommittee was not only picked up by the media; it aroused independent inquiries by the press as well. What the doctors had found could no longer be ignored. The *Washington Post* sent William Chapman to Mississippi, and he wrote back from Belzoni in the Delta:

> The absurd question is asked and Gussie Shaw explodes: "Of course the kids are hungry! Vernora, come and show the man."
> She lifts the blouse on the skinny 5-year-old girl and exposes, along with the frail chest, a stomach blotched with sores—"risings." Mrs. Shaw explains, "and the home remedy never did no good."[12]

A *Newsweek* article told of Cleosa Henley, a "black ruin of 46":

> He can't remember the last time he ate meat, other than pig's ears, hog jowls, or neck bones. Even relief cost money. Henley can buy $98 worth of Federal food stamps for $12—if he can ever put $12 together all at once. "I just ain't got that kinda money," says Henley, his gaze slowly dropping to his bare feet. "That money is right hard to git."[13]

Richard Strout of the *Christian Science Monitor* described the menu that Mississippi mother Hattie Jones Reed had planned for the day:

> There was oatmeal for breakfast with milk powder mixed with water. There was also rice, "though not enough of it." There was no lunch, but at three Mrs. Reed was fixing a corn-meal bread for supper. As a special treat, a relative had donated a squirrel. All four were looking forward hungrily to the squirrel.[14]

45

By the end of 1967, hunger was beginning to capture national attention. The issue had created some sense of urgency and was now at least on the political agenda. Nor did journalists and activists let up on their efforts to increase the public's concern about the hunger problem. Three new major undertakings fueled public outrage over government inaction: the Citizens' Board of Inquiry report, *Hunger U.S.A.* (1968); CBS's television documentary, "Hunger in America" (May 1968); and Nick Kotz's book, *Let Them Eat Promises* (1969).

The Citizens' Board of Inquiry grew out of the Citizens' Crusade Against Poverty, a liberal advocacy group formed in 1965. Even before Clark and Kennedy went to Mississippi, the group's director, Richard Boone, had proposed that the organization focus on the hunger issue. Funding was eventually obtained from the Field Foundation, and a Citizens' Board of Inquiry composed of prominent individuals was assembled. Assisted by an able staff, the board held hearings around the country and conducted extensive research on a wide range of hunger-related issues.

Hunger U.S.A., the one-hundred-page book produced by the Citizens' Board, offered an abundance of statistics and other data that detailed the extent of hunger and malnutrition in the United States.[15] It also included sickening photographs of starving children and adults. It even contained pictures of two Navajo infants in Arizona who were afflicted with Kwashiorkor, a disease caused by severe malnutrition that is more commonly found in undeveloped countries. Much of the report was written by Edgar Cahn and John Kramer, two lawyers who would continue to work against hunger in the years to come. Another member of the staff, Robert Choate, would later work on food programs for the Nixon administration.

Shortly after the publication of *Hunger, U.S.A.*, "Hunger in America" appeared on "CBS Reports." The May 21 broadcast, narrated by Charles Kuralt and produced by Don Hewitt, featured interviews with hungry poor people. The most devastating part of the show was the opening segment, when Kuralt described the following on the screen: "This baby is dying of starvation. He was an American. Now he is dead."[16] The program went on to criticize the food stamp program and the Department of Agriculture for their ineffectiveness in combatting hunger.

Nick Kotz, author of *Let Them Eat Promises*, began covering the hunger issue as a reporter for the Washington bureau of the *Des Moines Register*.[17] An aggressive reporter who developed an excellent set of contacts inside and outside USDA, Kotz wrote numerous articles about the condition of the hungry and poor in America. "I remember he came into my office once and said he was going to win a Pulitzer, with my cooperation," recalled one former high-ranking USDA official. Kotz was right: He won the Pulitzer Prize in 1968.

Let Them Eat Promises is an unremitting attack on Congress and the executive branch for their lack of commitment to ending hunger in America. Kotz emphasized the role that individual politicians and activists played in the conflict over food assistance legislation. On the one side were the "good guys," including Bobby Kennedy, Marian Wright, Robert Choate, and Leslie Dunbar. On the other side was evil—in particular, Representatives Jamie Whitten (D.–Miss.) and W. R. Poage (D.–Texas) and Senators James Eastland (D.–Miss.), Allen Ellender (D.–La), Spessard Holland (D.–Fla.), and John Stennis (D.–Miss.). Kotz portrayed them as prejudiced, uncaring, contemptible southern politicians.[18] He described many instances in which these men had used their powerful positions to thwart congressional initiative in the hunger area. Another villain was Secretary of Agriculture Orville Freeman. Though not prejudiced, Freeman rather was a coward for not standing up on the food issue to figures like Jamie Whitten, who chaired the House Appropriations subcommittee that oversaw the budget for USDA. In his own mind Kotz surely reserved a special place in Hell for Orville Freeman.

In addition to the intensified research and advocacy journalism, another important development was the emergence of a number of public interest lobbies to work on the food issue.[19] Collectively, these organizations became known as the "hunger lobby." They worked together, trying at various times to influence the Congress, the courts, the Agriculture Department, the White House, and the American public. In 1968 Richard Boone asked John Kramer if he would continue the effort begun with *Hunger U.S.A.* Kramer and Harvard professor Jean Mayer subsequently started the National Council on Hunger and Malnutrition. Earlier, Edgar Cahn had started his own group, the Citizens Advocate Center, in 1967. At Columbia University the Center for Social Welfare, Policy, and Law got involved in 1968, when it hired a young lawyer, Ron Pollack, who had just spent a summer in Mississippi. After he left USDA in 1969, Rod Leonard worked on food issues at the Children's Foundation before he started his own group, the Community Nutrition Institute.

Finally, the poor themselves began to lobby on their own behalf.

47

Indigenous leadership and organizations emerged as the poor became increasingly militant during the late 1960s.[20] One of the more notable endeavors was the Poor People's March on Washington in the spring of 1968, led by the Reverend Ralph Abernathy, successor to Martin Luther King, Jr., as head of the Southern Christian Leadership Conference. More than three thousand individuals marched into Washington and camped on the mall directly east of the Lincoln Memorial. "Resurrection City" was built opposite the Department of Agriculture buildings, and USDA became an immediate focus of the protesters. At an open meeting on May 23, Abernathy presented the group's demands to Secretary Freeman. The Johnson administration responded by making some small concessions, but no major reforms were initiated. Indeed, the administration was careful not to appear to concede too much, lest it seem to capitulate to the demonstrators.[21]

Journalists, legislators, lawyers, doctors, social activists, and the poor themselves had made hunger a prominent issue. A condition of widespread hunger and malnutrition had been proven to exist. Why, then, was nothing being done about it?

CONGRESS: NO CONSENSUS

Despite the increasing publicity surrounding the hunger issue, the Ninetieth Congress (1967–1968) failed to legislate food stamp reform. There are many reasons for this outcome. But above all, there was no consensus in Congress that substantial liberalization of the program was necessary. At the core of the opposition were key congressmen, including Whitten, House Agriculture Committee Chairman Poage, and Senate Agriculture Committee Chairman Ellender. Furthermore, a large group of conservative and moderate congressmen was opposed or unconcerned about food stamp reform. If congressmen are primarily motivated by constituent sentiment and the desire to be re-elected, then large numbers of congressmen sensed no widespread interest in their districts.[22] The press reports and apparent public outrage had not translated into constituency opinion intense enough to move a majority of congressmen from their own inclinations not to liberalize the program.[23]

A second important reason for the failure to achieve consensus was that the Johnson administration did not want extensive changes in food stamp policy. Liberalizing the program would cost more money, and the "guns or butter" dilemma caused by the Vietnam War led Johnson to resist increased appropriations for food stamps. Johnson himself made the decisions not to seek the funding necessary for reform.

Third, the substantial congressional and administrative opposition forced would-be reformers to concentrate on just winning enough of an appropriation to allow the program to expand into more areas of the country. Senators Kennedy, Clark, and Javits had taken strong positions in favor of food stamp reform, but coaxing a reform bill through both houses was another matter. In the House, even if Leonor Sullivan had wanted reform—which she did not—she had her hands full simply trying to get the program extended. To many House members the value of the food stamp legislation was still limited to its utility in logrolls with agriculture legislation. Only after leading a successful floor fight against a peanut subsidy was Mrs. Sullivan able to win a two-year, rather than a one-year, extension of the program in the fall of 1967.

Lastly, it is worth noting that some progress was being made. When Orville Freeman answered to individual congressmen or testified before various committees, he always cited statistics to show how the program was growing. Between 1966 and 1967 the number of projects more than doubled to 838, and there were always long lists of more to be opened in coming months. The members of USDA who had been subjected to criticism felt there was another side to the story, and they did not hesitate to try to publicize it. Although expansion of the program had nothing to do with structural reform, it did show Congress that something was being done. Expansion, therefore, served to divert congressional attention away from problems with the pricing and coupon allocation formulas. Expansion did not, of course, deter the criticisms of the growing hunger lobby. As Freeman lamented in a memo to the president, "hunger and malnutrition are easy to dramatize, progress to reduce it is not."[24]

Although Congress failed to pass any reform legislation during this time, it did have some influence on administrative reforms through regulation and instruction. The most significant arena for liberal efforts to reform the program was the new Senate Select Committee on Nutrition and Human Needs. The Clark subcommittee had held hearings in the summer of 1968 to consider a resolution to create a nutrition committee. Not surprisingly, they found a need for such a committee. The full Senate went along, and the select (temporary) committee was created, with George McGovern (D.–S.D.) appointed as chairman. After Robert Kennedy's assassination and Clark's defeat in the 1968 elections, McGovern became the leading Senate figure on nutrition and hunger policy. He chaired the Nutrition Committee until it fell victim to a Senate reorganization in 1977.

Through formal and informal means the Nutrition Committee maintained constant pressure on USDA. One of McGovern's greatest resources was a small but highly effective staff, and his total, unyielding commitment to expand government food assistance translated into great latitude for staff members. A succession of extremely capable and energetic aides—first William Smith, then Kenneth Schlossberg and Gerald Cassidy, and finally Marshall Matz—directed the committee's work. The Nutrition Committee did not have the authority to draft legislation. Rather, it was an investigative committee, and so it examined feeding programs and the quality of the American diet. The committee conducted numerous hearings on a wide range of questions relating to nutrition and governmental efforts to eradicate hunger. What the McGovern committee was really doing was performing legislative oversight—the responsibility that the Agriculture Committees were neglecting.

The Nutrition Committee was extremely skillful at using the media. Smith, Schlossberg, Cassidy, and Matz all had an excellent understanding of how a potential story could be framed so that it would appeal to the newspapers and the television networks. The press was their most valuable weapon, and it had to be used judiciously. One of the committee staffers explained how committee hearings were constructed:

> You have to understand, committee hearings are like a
> play. First, there's the plot. You need a controversial issue
> because news is controversy. Then there are the actors, you
> need some good guys and bad guys. You need a supporting
> cast, in this case the poor. The events, the hearings, they're
> the acts and subacts.

Committee staffers constantly searched for new ways to obtain press coverage. They cultivated their contacts in the press assiduously and became, in turn, contacts for reporters needing background for breaking stories.[25] The press became a surrogate for constituency pressure, making Congress and USDA a little more accountable.

50

THE ADMINISTRATION: GRUDGING INCREMENTALISM

As food stamp policy became increasingly controversial, administrators at the upper end of USDA's hierarchy had to pay more attention to the program. In contrast to the earlier years of the program, when Davis, Vanneman, and Kelley ran the operation with little outside interference, the secretary of agriculture and the president were now drawn into food stamp policy making. Another key figure during this time was Rodney Leonard. A speechwriter for Orville Freeman during Freeman's tenure as governor of Minnesota, Leonard had accompanied Freeman to Washington in 1961. After working on Freeman's staff, he was appointed as a deputy assistant secretary in 1965, and in 1968 he became administrator of the Consumer and Marketing Service. Howard Davis remained as deputy administrator for Consumer Food Programs, Sam Vanneman continued as Davis's deputy, and Isabelle Kelley also continued as director of the Food Stamp Division. Jim Springfield, a young political science graduate student, became Kelley's chief assistant.

Freeman, Leonard, Davis, and the others had hardly expected the onslaught of criticism and emotional charges that commenced with the Kennedy trip to Mississippi. For six years the program had seemed a success, with little dissatisfaction expressed on the part of the public or the Congress. The administrators felt that they had been flexible in adopting food stamp policy to the problems that emerged while, at the same time, remaining true to the original purposes of the program. As criticism mounted, they became highly defensive. Steiner writes that "the Department of Agriculture dedicated itself to documenting successes where there was no success."[26] Davis and Kelley particularly resented the charges. They knew that the food stamp program was being made a scapegoat for an inadequate welfare system. The real problem was government policy toward cash assistance. Moreover, the administrators for food stamps believed that the public's expectations of the program had outpaced real possibilities for reform. As one of them remarked years later, "No one told us that this was a program to feed *all* the poor."

One of the less defensive policy makers was Rod Leonard. When some members of USDA began to worry about the participation rate, Isabelle Kelley wrote a position paper on the purchase price for Leonard in February 1967. Kelley stressed the principle of the normal purchase expenditure requirement, and she complained that many critics still did not understand what the purchase price represented. After an objective review of the pros and cons of instituting various reforms, Kelley argued that the purchase price should not be reduced: "We do not believe the purpose of the Food Stamp Program should be perverted by shifting it toward a general welfare program for the poor."[27]

Rod Leonard did not regard the normal purchase concept with the same reverence that Davis and Kelley did. In a memo to Orville Freeman attached to Kelley's position paper, Leonard argued for a reduction in the purchase price to fifty cents per person per month for the poorest recipients, as opposed to the current two dollars. Leonard criticized the application of the normal purchase concept to the poorest of the poor: "Measuring family income at this level is like determining how much grain is left in an elevator after it has been emptied." Leonard recognized that decreasing the purchase price would increase the purely welfare aspect of the program; that is, it would free those dollars normally used for food. He brushed aside this objection, however, telling Freeman that "the real issue is not whether Food Stamps is a welfare program, but the kind of welfare program it should be. . . ."[28] Freeman remained unmoved and decided against any change.

Less than two months later, however, Freeman would find himself under intense scrutiny because of the Clark subcommittee trip to Mississippi. After he met with Kennedy and Clark upon their return, Freeman sent Howard Davis and another aide, William Seabron, on a fact-finding mission to Mississippi. Davis, angry at what he considered unwarranted political interference by Senator Kennedy, believed the criticism to be unfair, since commodity or food stamp programs were available in all eighty-two counties of Mississippi. Together with Marian Wright and Kennedy aide Peter Edelman, Davis and Seabron retraced Kennedy's and Clark's steps in the Delta. Viewing the unyielding poverty, Davis knew that politically he was beaten. Although it was AFDC that needed the most serious reform, he recognized that the food stamp purchase price would eventually have to bow to political realities. When Davis and Seabron returned to Washington, they were debriefed by Freeman legislative aide Ken Birkhead. Based on their report, Birkhead told Freeman that "much of what Senators Clark and Kennedy found is true."[29] Yet Freeman still hesitated to change the administrative guidelines on the purchase price. On the same day he received Birkhead's memorandum, Freeman called Johnson domestic adviser Joseph Califano and told him that he did not want to move to a lower purchase price because it might jeopardize the already vulnerable bill to extend the food stamp program.[30]

Pressure on Freeman to do something about food stamp reform continued, however, and Rod Leonard kept urging him to approve the fifty-cent purchase price. Freeman sent Ken Birkhead to Jamie Whitten to try to clear a move to the fifty-cent minimum. Whitten equivocated, but told Birkhead the whole program was in trouble in Congress. House Agriculture Committee Chairman Poage represented an even bigger problem, since he openly opposed a drop in the minimum purchase price.

By the end of June, Freeman finally decided to act without the support of Whitten and Poage, but he found himself in an untenable position. Not only would he have to testify at upcoming hearings of the Clark subcommittee, but he had also agreed to go to Mississippi to examine some rural development projects. Whatever decision he made, he was going to anger somebody. On June 26, the day he flew to Mississippi, changes in the purchase price were announced, giving Freeman some small reforms to offer to the local civil rights leaders with whom he would meet. The new purchase and allotment tables, issued through program instructions, dropped the purchase price to fifty cents per person for families with incomes below thirty dollars a month. The new tables reduced the purchase price by a few dollars for most other families as well.[31]

Howard Davis and Isabelle Kelley had reconciled themselves to the debasement of the normal purchase requirement principle. They knew, however, that the decrease in the purchase price would not dramatically increase participation. Their figures had consistently shown that nonparticipation was greatest among those at the higher, not the lower, end of the income scale. But the decision had been made, and implementation of the new pricing tables went smoothly as most states adopted them quickly.

Criticism of the program abated in the fall and winter, but by the spring of 1968, USDA was on the defensive again with the publication of *Hunger U.S.A.* Calls for food stamp reform were renewed. Feasible reform options for the program fell into two categories. First, there could be an overall liberalization of the basis of issuance tables with an increase in coupon allocations, a reduction in purchase prices, or both. This alternative would cost a substantial amount of money. A second possibility was to give free stamps to recipients with less than thirty dollars a month in family income, a plan that would only cost around $5 million a year. Although this reform would be of little help to the large majority of recipients, free stamps for some would have tremendous symbolic value.

If comprehensive liberalization of the basis of issuance tables were to be accomplished, more money would have to be forthcoming from the Congress. Through the spring and summer of 1968 a number of proposals to expand the program were presented to President Johnson. Two hundred twenty-five million dollars was already authorized for fiscal year 1969, and the administration publically backed a $20 million increase. A working group composed of Freeman, Califano, Assistant Director of the Bureau of the Budget Charles Zwick, and White House staffers Charles Murphy, DeVier Pierson, and James Gaither recommended to Johnson in late June that he back an enlarged budget request for $415 million. This extra $170 million would permit rapid expansion into 250 counties waiting to join the program, provide free stamps to the very poorest, reduce the purchase price to all other recipients, and create a liberal, national eligibility (income ceiling) standard. Johnson rejected the proposal. A few days later a less ambitious package presented to the president asked for a $130 million increase. The president, desperately trying to keep the domestic side of the budget down because of the cost of the Vietnam War, rejected this request as well.[32]

As it turned out, the controversy over the food stamp program allowed Congresswoman Sullivan to win a $315 million authorization for fiscal year 1969. Although the administration did not back the increase, USDA used the extra money to liberalize the basis of issuance tables. Through a combination of modest increases in the allotments and modest decreases in the amount of the purchase price, food stamps were made a little bit of a better bargain.

The other major reform option—to give free stamps to the poorest recipients—received no impetus from the increased appropriation. There was little sentiment inside USDA for such a move. Davis and Kelley preferred to keep the vestige of the normal purchase requirement with the fifty-cent charge. Freeman was not particularly enthusiastic about the idea of free stamps, but he would have gone along if it had received support in Congress. At one point Rod Leonard asked

Leonor Sullivan if she would back such a move. She told Leonard in no uncertain terms that everybody, no matter how poor, had to pay something for their stamps, even if it was only a token fifty cents. Knowing Poage's and Whitten's attitude, Freeman felt that it would be unwise to go ahead without Congresswoman Sullivan's backing. The minimum charge continued.

There was no shortage of critics to decry USDA's decision not to provide free stamps for the neediest. Free stamps even became something of a rallying cry for the hunger lobby. The department consistently responded that it had no choice but to charge for the stamps because a section of the original law required that participants pay their normal expenditures for their stamps. But everyone concerned knew that USDA could make the change if it wanted to. As one official put it, "When people had so low and irregular an income, they're not spending a 'normal' amount." Moreover, the USDA counsel's office did not interpret the legislative history as requiring a cash purchase from those who had little, if any, income.[33] The real stumbling block was Leonor Sullivan, whose value to the program made Freeman think twice about taking an action with which she disagreed. Congresswoman Sullivan had repeatedly stated that a token purchase price allowed the poorest recipients some dignity, in as much as they were buying, as opposed to being given, their food stamps. "I guess fifty cents was what dignity was worth in those days," mused one of her opponents on the issue.

By the time the Johnson administration left office in January 1969, it had gone only a short distance toward meeting the demands of the hunger lobby. Two small sets of changes in the basis of issuance tables had been made, somewhat grudgingly, during the two years of conflict over the program. Both political appointees and career civil servants became highly defensive about what they thought was a well-run and well-designed program. They were constantly angered by charges they knew to be exaggerated. They, too, cared about the hungry in America, and they never understood how they could be so unfairly criticized by the media and the hunger lobby. As one target of the hunger lobby's assault later commented, "It was terribly hard for us to be the bad guys. We had worked all our professional lives to feed needy people and nobody cared. Then hunger becomes an issue and it was a case of everywhere we went, 'Here comes that stinking Department of Agriculture.'"

HOW REGULATIONS ARE WRITTEN:
INCENTIVES FOR INTERVENTION

The last years of the Johnson administration witnessed a depressing failure of the federal government to take responsibility for a program that was badly in need of reform. Career bureaucrats in USDA continued to believe that the food stamp program was operating as it should. The program's cost, rather than its performance, appeared to be the White House's only concern. For its part, Congress remained largely indifferent. A general lack of interest permitted a few conservative committee chairmen to stand in the way of reform legislation.

Congress's failure to amend substantially the Food Stamp Act of 1964 may seem to be a classic case of neglect of its oversight responsibilities. A program authorized by the House and the Senate was not fulfilling its expectations. Congress nevertheless refused to act to change the law that embodied these unsuccessful policies. Consequently, administrators retained the discretion to implement the program according to their original, flawed design.

It would be unfair, however, to interpret Congress's actions during 1967 and 1968 as wholly inadequate. Although most legislators still cared little about food stamps, for the first time some members of Congress other than Leonor Sullivan were beginning to show an interest in the program. A number of congressmen finally began to question the judgment of Freeman, Davis, and other USDA officials.

The activities of a handful of legislators, especially those of Senators Kennedy, Clark, and McGovern, should not be dismissed as symbolic gestures amid general congressional apathy. These individuals, along with their allies in interest groups and in the media, accomplished a great deal. They brought the program's problems out of the dark by making food stamps a nationally recognized issue. The senators also began to establish an important pattern in the development of the food stamp program. Starting in 1967, USDA officials found themselves under pressure from congressmen who actively sought to influence administrative policy making. By means of the field trip to Mississippi, hearings, and private communications, congressmen were trying to force USDA to adopt more generous price and benefit guidelines.

Despite the lack of success in the short run, the efforts of these senators to attain policy goals through intervention into the administrative process was a logical strategy. It was highly unlikely that reform legislation could get through both Agriculture Committees and both houses. By engaging instead in a tug of war with USDA, where Freeman and his aides could be put on the defensive, there was at least some chance that the program could be liberalized through regulations and guidelines. The tactic might be described as an "appeals court strategy": When a legislator sees diminishing returns in pushing for statutory reform, he or she will find that it often makes sense to expend available time and energy upon lobbying the relevant agency for administrative changes in the program at issue.

Legislative intervention in the administrative process would continue to play a significant role in food stamp policy making. A fundamental question in regard to legislative intervention is: What were the incentives that prompted a few legislators to become involved in trying to influence USDA policy making on food stamps?

Clearly, these senators responded in some degree to the political (largely re-election) goals that motivate all congressmen. There was publicity and recognition available, precious commodities to be sure. Interest groups requested help, and their gratitude could be obtained as well. Even if the majority of congressmen saw little at stake with the food stamp program, a few considered the issue to be worthy of the investment of their time.

The re-election goal has been cited by David Mayhew as the primary incentive for intervention with the bureaucracy. In *Congress: The Electoral Connection*, Mayhew argues compellingly that legislators "intervene effectively in the bureaucracy on matters where they can claim credit for intervention."[34] If credit—the belief by appreciative constituents and client groups that a legislator has affected governmental policy—is not likely to be obtained on an issue, then it is irrational for a congressman to devote his time on such activities. It seems reasonable to conclude that the more credit available on an issue, the greater the incentive to intervene.

Yet Mayhew's explanation really begs the question. There is some credit to be gained in almost all policy areas. On practically any given matter, a congressman can pursue intervention, for whatever reasons, with the assurance that some audience will be grateful. And although it is true that some issues offer more potential for credit than others, it is also true that congressmen do not concentrate their intervention on the most prominent issue of the month or year. Congressmen have a wide choice of issues where credit can be gained.

In terms of understanding the motives for legislative intervention,

Mayhew's credit-claiming thesis is incomplete. It would be far too cynical to attribute the activities of Kennedy, Clark, and McGovern solely to that impulse. Their lobbying of USDA sprang from a more complex set of incentives. At the core of their efforts was surely a view of the political world that impelled them to work on behalf of society's underclass. There must be other reasons for their behavior as well. The task that lies ahead in this analysis of the food stamp program is to build a more comprehensive explanation of why congressmen seek to influence the writing of regulations and guidelines in administrative agencies.

3

REFORM THROUGH
REGULATION

A LTHOUGH RICHARD NIXON'S FIRST
term as president is more remembered for his
achievements in foreign policy, his administration made some imaginative efforts on the domestic side as well. Among the domestic policy proposals was a sweeping welfare reform plan. Had it been enacted, Nixon's Family Assistance Plan would have created a guaranteed annual income for all Americans. This proposal was designed to replace the various basic welfare programs, including food stamps, with one comprehensive program of cash assistance. Congress defeated the Family Assistance Plan, but the changes the administration was able to institute in the food stamp program played an important part in making the welfare system more generous and more accessible.

REPUBLICAN INITIATIVE

Richard Nixon was highly aware of the hunger problem when he took office. In an address to four hundred or so USDA officials during his get-acquainted call a few weeks after the inauguration, he focused on the hunger issue, not farm policy. Nixon spoke movingly of the challenge facing the department and specifically mentioned CBS's "Hunger in America," noting that "millions of Americans saw on television that in this rich land, there is hunger."[1]

With substantial public pressure to do something about hunger, and with the congressional authorization for the food stamp program soon to run out, the job of preparing an administration response to the hunger issue fell to the newly created Urban Affairs Council. A White House advisory body patterned after the National Security Council, the Urban Affairs Council was designed to be a policy planning staff for

59

domestic issues. Its membership included the relevant Cabinet secretaries, and its staff was headed by Harvard University professor Daniel Patrick Moynihan. The hunger problem was the responsibility of the council's subcommittee on Food and Nutrition, headed by the new secretary of agriculture, Clifford Hardin. Hardin, an agricultural economist, depended heavily upon his assistant secretary for Consumer and Marketing Services, Richard Lyng, in formulating food stamp policy. For his part, Lyng drew upon a staff composed of individuals from the White House, the Department of Health, Education, and Welfare (HEW), and his own Department of Agriculture. Within USDA, Lyng's primary resource people were Howard Davis, Isabelle Kelley, and Jim Springfield.

The staff worked rapidly to prepare a report for the full Urban Affairs Council. They did not try to minimize the scope of the hunger problem. Based on the nutritional data available, the staff report concluded that one-half of the poor in the South and 20 percent of the poor in the North were malnourished. They also stated that 5 to 10 million Americans suffered from "severe" hunger and malnutrition.[2] The report was surprisingly blunt about the failures of the food stamp program, indicating that "current payment and value schedules are inequitable and appear to strongly discourage participation." It noted that many people "cannot affort to buy into the program" and that those in extreme poverty were receiving stamps worth only 60 percent of their minimum nutritional needs.[3]

Davis and Kelley did not control what went into the report, but in any case they were now much less defensive about the food stamp program. Both were eager to help the new administration and, in particular, their immediate superior, Richard Lyng. Although a mistrust of career civil servants would gradually pervade the upper reaches of the Nixon administration, Lyng had no reservations about his staff's loyalty, and he came to depend upon these careerists quite heavily.[4]

The members of the Urban Affairs Council task force recommended a set of food stamp reform proposals that would cost an additional $1.7 billion.The provisions of their package included raising the allotments of all recipients to the level of USDA's cheapest nutritious diet plan (then $100 a month for a family of four), fixing a maximum price ceiling for the stamps at 30 percent of a family's income, providing free stamps for families with incomes under $50 a month, and setting national eligibility standards to replace the patchwork system of individual state standards.[5] The report was presented to the full Urban

Affairs Council in mid-March, only two months after Nixon had taken office. The president attended this meeting, and Hardin pushed Nixon to make a commitment, emphasizing, "There is great urgency about this. This is the hottest item on the domestic front, and we must take the leadership ourselves."[6] However, the committee plan, outlined by Lyng, ran into immediate attack from Arthur Burns, the president's conservative adviser for domestic affairs, who believed that the hunger problem was exaggerated. A strong ally of Burns was Budget Director Robert Mayo, who, in the words of one administration official, was "death on food stamps."

After hearing the arguments of Lyng and Burns, the president declined to make a firm decision.[7] Nixon seemed most disturbed about the cost of the program. During the meeting he asked Lyng what it would cost if all counties in the United States were given a food stamp program. Nixon was openly taken aback by Lyng's reply that the figure would be somewhere in the neighborhood of $3.5 to $4 billion a year. The next month and a half saw more meetings of the Urban Affairs Council. Hardin continued to press for food stamp reform, and Burns and Mayo staunchly continued to oppose it.

However, the major battle within the administration was not over food stamps but over Daniel Moynihan's proposed Family Assistance Plan (FAP). FAP would have implemented a negative income tax system to replace AFDC and other cash assistance programs. Nixon's initial attitude on FAP was ambivalent. He liked the idea of replacing tired, old Democratic programs that did not work, but he resisted proposing any scheme that would significantly increase government expenditures on welfare. Moreover, his attitude toward the poor remained suspicious. As one Nixon aide observed, "One day he'd be impressed by what Pat [Moynihan] said. Then the next day, he'd be pissed off about what some little congressman had told him about welfare cheats."

Nixon's ambivalence was also reflected in his indecision over liberalization of the food stamp program. Soon, however, it appeared that, although Nixon would back FAP, Burns and Mayo would have their way on food stamps. Reports circulated in the press that Nexon had rejected plans to increase spending on government food programs substantially. Robert Choate, who had joined the administration as a consultant on nutrition, quit, believing that Nixon had no intention of backing major reforms in the food area.

George McGovern and his aides on the Nutrition Committee were not going to let Nixon off without a fight. They had been trying to goad the administration into action from the very beginning of the term. McGovern and Senator Ernest Hollings, who had recently returned from a hunger inspection tour of his native South Carolina, met privately with Hardin in February and persuaded him to try a zero purchase price in some food stamp projects.[8] Now, with Nixon's apparent decision not to go ahead with food stamp reform, progress seemed to be coming to a halt. McGovern had already arranged for an appearance by Hardin and HEW Secretary Robert Finch before the Nutrition Committee when word of Nixon's decision surfaced in the press. To increase the pressure on Hardin and Finch, McGovern and his aides leaked a copy of the Urban Affairs Council report to the *Washington Post* a few days before their testimony on May 7.[9]

The scheduled appearance of Hardin and Finch forced the administration's hands. The two Cabinet secretaries were placed in the untenable position of having to defend publicly a program that their own research had found to be inadequate. In this embarrassing situation, Nixon, at the last minute, relented. A decision was made to move forcefully on the hunger issue.[10] The day before Hardin's and Finch's committee appearance, Nixon sent a message to Congress outlining a billion-dollar increase in funding for food programs. It was an eloquent plea for congressional action. In conclusion, Nixon said that "the moment is at hand to put an end to hunger in America itself for all time."[11]

The Nixon bill generally followed the recommendations of the Urban Affairs Council report. In addition to his legislative proposal, Nixon declared that there would be a White House Conference on Food, Nutrition, and Health, scheduled for December 1969. In September the Senate passed a food stamp reform bill that provided for allotment schedules even more generous than the level of the lowest-cost economy food plan, which was backed by the Urban Affairs Council. The House, however, once again proved to be the stumbling block for the food stamp program. Agriculture Committee Chairman W. R. Poage successfully bottled up the food stamp bill, hoping to use it for logrolling purposes when the farm bill expired the next year. As the conference date approached and the administration still had no food stamp reform passed, the White House began to fear that the conference would turn into a forum for critics of the administration's food policy. Administration officials already suspected that nutritionist Jean Mayer, the conference's chairman, was not doing his best to protect the White House from potential embarrassment during the planning of the conference.[12]

For the second time in a year the threat of adverse reports in the press spurred the White House into action on the food stamp issue. On the day before the president was to address the conference, Hardin announced that USDA was instituting some major reforms through administrative action. Most important, coupon allotments would be set, regardless of family income, at the level of the economy diet plan.[13] To make the program even more attractive, the purchase price would also decline for the vast majority of recipients. Most families would pay no more than 25 percent of their income for their stamps. A family of four with an income of $50 a month, for example, was then paying $20 to get $64 worth of stamps. Under the Hardin reforms, the same family would pay $10 and receive $106 in stamps. Hardin also announced the rapid expansion of the program into areas that had neither a food stamp nor a commodity program and the institution of an outreach effort to locate and educate nonparticipants where programs existed.

This combination of increased allotments and decreased purchase prices was the most significant change ever made in the history of the program. It came at a time when the House had failed to pass a bill that proposed much the same reforms. Hardin used as a legislative pretext a simple authorization (which included no program changes) and a subsequent appropriation raising food stamps funds to $610 million for fiscal year 1970. This was hardly a solid legislative basis for Hardin's actions. The increased authorization was not an expression of congressional intent or sentiment for any specific changes other than the obvious expansion of the program into new areas. Hardin claimed only a general authority and never alleged that the money was intended for the specific purposes to which he put it. It was, as one Republican representative called it, "legislation on an appropriation."

Hardin did seek some informal clearance for his administrative reforms. The Senate, of course, presented no problem, since it had already passed a bill with provisions more liberal than those Hardin had instituted. In the House he talked to Poage and Whitten. Neither of them favored the reforms, but they were faced with something of a *fait accompli*. Trying to stop Hardin would mean becoming public villains on the issue, with excoriation from the hunger lobby and the press assured. Opposition would also mean standing in the way of a new administration with which, philosophically, they were generally in tune.

63

Poage certainly could stand up to criticism, but he had begun to tire of the food stamp conflict. He was worried as well about his committee, where support had begun to develop for some type of food stamp reform. He did not want to have to deal with any open conflict in the Agriculture Committee.[14] Going along with Hardin's reforms was, in one committee member's words, "better than a bloodletting." Although they may not have given their formal blessing, Poage and Whitten remained silent.

Finally, after over two years of concerted effort, the work of the antihunger activists had paid off. A conservative president had agreed to administrative changes that produced a major liberalization of the program. By bringing all recipients up to the allotment level of the economy food plan, the food stamp program for the first time guaranteed its participants enough coupons to purchase a nutritionally adequate diet.

FAP AND FOOD STAMPS

At the same time that the White House was backing food stamp reform, it continued to examine Daniel Moynihan's proposal for a guaranteed annual income. On August 8, 1969, President Nixon went on national television to tell the American public about the Family Assistance Plan. In retrospect, it is clear that the existence of the food stamp program, which was developed because of the shortcomings of the welfare system, contributed to the defeat of FAP, a program designed to alleviate the ills of that very system. One can only speculate as to what would have happened to FAP had no food stamp program existed. Nevertheless, the fact that millions of welfare recipients were entitled to cash assistance *plus* food stamps, while millions of others on welfare received no stamps, made it enormously difficult to come up with a plan that had benefit levels satisfactory to all parties concerned. It is important to understand the principles of FAP and the reasons for its defeat in order properly to appreciate food stamp reform.[15]

The primary target of FAP was AFDC, the most expensive of the welfare programs to be consolidated. AFDC was created as a small part of the 1935 Social Security Act in order to aid destitute families that no longer had a male breadwinner. By 1950 it had grown slowly to 2.2 million participants. In 1969 the AFDC rolls averaged 6.7 million individuals, and there was a sharp rise to over 10 million recipients by 1972. AFDC has been criticized on a number of grounds. To begin with, benefit levels are different in each state, and the disparities between states are great. These disparities are caused more by differences in available resources and in ideology than by differences in the standards of living in each state. AFDC is considered anti-family because some states do not offer support to families with an unemployed father in the household and thus seemingly encourage a father to leave home so that his wife and children can receive welfare. Conservatives still condemn the program for not having stronger work requirements. Liberals fault the program for not providing greater work-training opportunities.

FAP would have been funded entirely by the federal government rather than by the matching federal-state funds that support AFDC. Eligibility was to be based on a single national standard, and benefits would be set at a guaranteed annual level. The incentive to work would be preserved, despite the guaranteed income, by the use of a "negative income tax" system. If, for example, the eligibility line is $3,000 a year for a family of four, the federal government *guarantees* cash assistance of $3,000 for each family. If a family is receiving its $3,000 from the government, its members still have good reason to find work, because any outside money they earn will be subject to a liberal benefit reduction rate. In the case of FAP, the benefit reduction rate was 50 percent. That is, for every dollar earned, the welfare payment is reduced by fifty cents. If a family receiving the guaranteed income earns an additional $2,000 through one or more jobs, it will end up with an income of $4,000 ($2,000 from work plus $2,000 in net—after "tax"—guaranteed annual income).

The original FAP proposal presented to the Congress called for a guaranteed annual income of $1,600 a year for a family of four. As a further work incentive, FAP included a $60 a month ($720 a year) work disregard. The work disregard allowed the first $60 a month in outside income to be earned with no benefit reduction in the guaranteed annual income. Since $1,600 a year was much less than many northern states paid in AFDC benefits, the Nixon administration expressed an optimistic expectation that these states would supplement the FAP payment so that their welfare recipients would not suffer any loss of income.

A critical factor in the computation of this guaranteed annual income was how food stamps were figured into the equation. In some northern states a family could have an income of over $2,500 in combined cash assistance and food stamps. Whether or not future recipients under FAP could also receive food stamps would make a big difference in reducing the gap between the proposed $1,600 income floor and the current payments to joint AFDC–food stamp participants in certain northern states. Three alternatives on food stamps were open to the FAP planners. First, they could allow families on FAP to purchase food stamps with part of their cash payment. Under allocation tables proposed by the administration in May 1969, a family of four with no outside income could use $480 of its FAP payment to buy $1,200 in food stamps. The family's net amount of income and stamps would be $2,320, considerably more generous than the flat $1,600 annual benefit. A second option was to give FAP recipients a cash equivalent of the amount of bonus stamps for which they were eligible. Thus, the same family would receive $2,320 in cash, without the bother of having to buy and use stamps. A third alternative was to keep the benefit level at a strict $1,600, with no concomitant food stamp eligibility.[16]

Despite the importance of the role of food stamps in the Family Assistance Plan, it was treated as an incidental matter. For some inexplicable reason, planners never regarded the food stamp question as fundamental to the basic structure of FAP. Looking back, one of those who helped to design FAP admitted, "Nobody really understood the relationship of food stamps to FAP." As it turned out, the decision was not made until the very end. On the day after the president's television address, the FAP working group met in the office of presidential domestic adviser John Ehrlichman. Members of the working group would meet shortly with the press to brief them on the details of the president's proposal. Nixon had said nothing in his speech about food stamps. One of the participants in the meeting describes what happened:

> It had not been decided still as to what we were going to
> do with food stamps. Robert Patricelli asked Ehrlichman if food
> stamps would be part of the plan. Ehrlichman told Patricelli
> "No," it had been cashed out. There would be no food stamps. He
> was emphatic and instructed Patricelli to say there would be
> no food stamps if asked the question.

At the ensuing press conference reporter Nick Kotz, who had just finished *Let Them Eat Promises*, brought up the food stamp issue. He directed his initial question about food stamps and the new program at

Richard Nathan, assistant director of the Bureau of the Budget. Nathan faithfully answered the question in line with Ehrlichman's instructions. "That's when the shit hit the fan," recalled one who was present. Kotz was incensed at the idea of abolishing food stamps without any cash equivalency added to the FAP payment. Rather pointed and antagonistic questions followed on food stamps, and Moynihan, FAP's chief architect, began to worry about how the press was going to treat the issue. He tried to soften Nathan's answer by saying that the system would be refined so that no one would really lose benefits. The damage had been done, however, and the administration found itself immediately on the defensive on the food stamp issue.

The attack on FAP by food stamp advocates was lead by John Kramer of the Council on Hunger and Malnutrition. Kramer charged that millions of welfare recipients would be worse off under an FAP system with no food stamps, and he excoriated the Family Assistance Plan as the "Family Deprivation System."[17] Within the administration, Jean Mayer lobbied furiously for a restoration of food stamps. Mayer knew that the upcoming White House conference would be a fiasco if food stamps were not a part of the FAP proposal. The White House initially resisted, wanting to hold down the overall cost of FAP to keep it acceptable to conservatives. It reaffirmed the no food stamps decision a week after the press conference. But the force of public opinion and the possible loss of liberal support for FAP soon made Nixon change his mind. Once again, the imminent appearance of Hardin and Finch before the Nutrition Committee precipitated the White House decision. If enacted, FAP would now permit recipients to use a portion of their money to purchase food stamps.

FAP could never escape the dilemma of having to appeal to both liberals and conservatives. Some conservatives objected primarily to the cost, but many remained unalterably opposed to the whole idea of a guaranteed annual income. Senator Russell Long (D.–La.), whose Finance Committee had jurisdiction over FAP, called the proposal a "welfare expansion and mess perpetuation bill."[18] Liberals remained unconvinced that the more generous AFDC states would supplement FAP so that participants would not be worse off under the new program. Although FAP passed the House, it could not get through the Senate. By October 1972, FAP was dead.

For many, the fight over FAP had obscured food stamp reform. In fact, *food stamps had come to resemble a guaranteed annual income.* The December 1969 administrative reforms had made benefits equal throughout the country. Eligibility was based solely on income and assets. Both the nonworking and the working poor could qualify, and a liberal benefit reduction rate of 30 percent preserved the incentive to work. The costs of the benefits provided to recipients was borne totally by the federal government. Food stamps had turned into what Richard Nathan later called a "mini-negative income tax."[19] FAP had been killed, but not welfare reform.

Welfare reform had been achieved through administrative changes in the food stamp program.

THE 1971 REGULATIONS

After years of controversy and indecision, the Congress finally passed a food stamp reform bill on the last day of 1970.[20] Passage of the bill was somewhat anticlimactic in light of the Hardin administrative reforms that had been implemented earlier in the year. As one Capitol Hill staffer later said, "The 1970 act was really the congressional stamp of approval over what the Department had already done." Indeed, the new legislation put into statute the requirement that families be given enough coupons to purchase a nutritionally adequate diet (the economy food plan), placed an absolute ceiling on the purchase price at 30 percent of a family's income, and even reiterated Hardin's pledge of an outreach program. The law did go beyond the regulations in specifically permitting free food stamps for families with less than thirty dollars a month in income. The free food stamp experiment had not been extended beyond the two South Carolina projects, and despite the long fight over this issue, it was not as important as the other reforms. Participation was already relatively high at the lower end of the scale, where the fifty-cent per person price was in effect.

The 1970 law did contain one significant new reform. A provision of the legislation called for national standards of eligibility. No longer would a family's eligibility be determined by the income limits of a state's AFDC program. No longer would it be more difficult to qualify for the program in Mississippi than in New York.

Like the administrative reforms that preceded this 1970 act, the administrative regulations that grew out of it embodied important policy decisions. Issued in 1971, these regulations were the first food stamp policy changes to be put through the notice and comment process. Over the years Howard Davis and Isabelle Kelley had limited the number of formal regulations proposed and published in the *Federal Register* because they preferred to keep their working options flexible. The lack of notice and comment on most administrative guidelines was also a reflection of their tight control over the program during its early years.

The subjection of new food stamp regulations to the formal rule-making process at this time can be explained in four ways. First, the creation of national income eligibility standards allowed administrators for the first time to formulate a single price and allocation table for each family size for the entire country. The most crucial of all administrative guidelines was no longer a matter for each state to determine. The law now made it practical to write rules of national applicability for many policies where, earlier, that had not been feasible.

Second, USDA, as well as other government agencies and departments, was coming into compliance with a review commission's recommendation that rulemaking procedures be used in policy areas exempted under the Administrative Procedure Act, specifically in matters relating to "public property, loans, grants, benefits or contracts." As a welfare benefit, food stamp allocation guidelines had fallen outside of the law.[21] USDA now extended the scope of the Administrative Procedure Act to include grants, benefits, and the like.

Third, the rapidly developing public interest law movement made USDA officials increasingly sensitive to the need for a solid legal foundation for their administrative guidelines.[22] The hunger lobby had no qualms about taking the department to court. Putting guidelines through notice and comment and making them part of the *Code of Federal Regulations* would give the Agriculture Department added protection against legal challenges to its program operations.

Fourth, regulations became more prevalent because of a growth in the bureaucracy that administered the program. In 1969 a separate agency, the Food and Nutrition Service (FNS), was established to oversee food stamps, commodity distribution, school lunch, school breakfast, and other feeding programs. By that year the food stamp program had expanded to 1,489 projects—almost one in every other county in the United States. As the program and its bureaucracy became more complex, so did its decision-making routines. The increasing bureaucratization of the food stamp operation in Washington contributed to a greater tendency to use the more structured notice and comment process.

As the first administrator of FNS, President Nixon appointed Edward J. Hekman, who had previously headed the Keebler Company, a large biscuit manufacturing concern. Howard Davis continued as Hekman's deputy administrator. When Sam Vanneman retired in 1970, Isabelle Kelley took his place in the administrator's office, and Jim Springfield replaced Kelley as head of FNS's Food Stamp Division.

The writing of the regulations for the 1970 law began when Jim Springfield took its legislative history home for a week's vacation. After reading the legislation through, Springfield mapped out a plan for coordinating the writing of the regulations. Although the guidelines were now to be written for the *Federal Register*, USDA lawyers would not be involved in their actual drafting. Regulations would continue to be written within FNS by the specialists who had authority over various aspects of the program.

The most critical regulations to be formulated had to do with the new income eligibility standard. An understanding already existed between the Agriculture Committees and FNS that the income eligibility line would be 3.3 times the amount of the coupon allocation, which the Hardin reforms had already set at the cost of the economy food plan. Fixing the income line at 3.3 times the cost of the economy food plan reflected the ability of families over the line to purchase an adequate diet for less than 30 percent of their current income. There was little extended analysis of the application of the 30 percent standard to the national income eligibility line. Since the informal understanding had made congressional intent clear, Springfield was not burdened with a decision on this issue. At the time, the economy diet cost $108, so the income limit for a family of four was set at $360 a month ($4,320 a year).[23]

A somewhat more difficult question for Springfield and his aides was how to define income. Owing to the system of shelter and other deductions, income had been traditionally defined as *net* income—the amount left over after the deductions were subtracted. Of the deductions allowed, the shelter deduction was by far the most important. Removing it would effecitvely mean a price increase for many who were now able to deduct the portion of their shelter costs that was over 30 percent of their income.[24] On the question of what, if any, deductions were to be allowed, there was no obvious congressional intent, primarily because the members of the Agriculture Committees seemed to have no working knowledge of the way income was determined in the program. Few members had ever looked into the program with any real interest.

Given the lack of any written intent or informal understanding on the problem of income deductions, Springfield and his colleagues had an open choice as to what they wanted to do. "We had no guidelines," said one of the administrators. "There was virtually no communication between the Congress and us on the '71 regulations. None." Springfield and a working group of half a dozen others decided to continue the practice of allowing deductions for excessive shelter costs, emergency expenditures, unusual medical expenses, and child care. Any mandatory payroll deductions or union dues taken out of a paycheck would, as before, be disregarded as income. Since they were only reaffirming existing policy, there seemed little reason to drop these deductions. A more troublesome decision was whether or not to include a work incentive deduction. A point of comparison was AFDC, which had been amended so that the first thirty dollars of income earned from a job and one-third of any income thereafter would not be held liable for any benefit reduction. Should the food stamp program also adopt a work disregard, so that recipients would have a greater incentive to find a job and break out of the cycle of poverty? The Springfield group decided against a work deduction. They felt that an added work incentive beyond the liberal benefit reduction rate in the price and allocation tables would be an unreasonable change in the nature of the program. Its purpose was to provide supplementary food; it was not intended as a parallel to AFDC.

One sticky issue remained. Conservatives in the Congress had been successful in writing into the law a work registration requirement, which reflected the widespread belief that all able-bodied adults (excluding mothers with small children) should be willing to search for jobs and accept offers of employment. If they refused offers of employment, then they should be removed from the program. The work requirement was a personal victory for Chairman Poage, who had been a forceful advocate of a tough job-search provision.

The administrators of the food stamp program felt that the only efficient way to handle work registration was through the existing job-training and job-search programs of the Department of Labor. As a result, Agriculture gave responsibility for running its job searches to the Labor's Employment Services Administration. Since that department's own programs required individuals to take jobs of "suitable" employment, FNS regulations also specified that food stamp recipients take jobs "suitable" in terms of their experience. Poage and other convervatives were irate at this weak work registration regulation. They felt that able-bodied adults should have to take *any* job offered to them or be thrown out of the program. Poage and his allies would have liked to have had more precise language in the law or legislative report, but there was no consensus on how far the work registration requirement should go. Still, they believed that committee intent was clear and that FNS was circumventing that intent by putting a giant loophole in the regulations.

The regulations, which ran to nineteen pages, were published in their proposed form on April 16. Conservatives in Congress were not alone in finding fault with their content. Antihunger activists had hoped for a number of policy changes that did not appear. Ron Pollack, head of the newly founded Food Research and Action Center, Kenneth Schlossberg and Gerald Cassidy of the Senate Nutrition Committee, and others had met with Jim Springfield and Isabelle Kelley while the regulations were being formulated to offer drafts of proposed regulations. Although members of the hunger lobby were pleased at the language of the work requirement, they found little else to cheer about.

Pollack, Rod Leonard (who had just started the Community Nutrition Institute), Schlossberg, and Cassidy met with state food stamp administrators and other food stamp activists to plot their strategy. Schlossberg and Cassidy favored a plan to have the Nutrition Committee hold hearings on the regulations. The others eagerly accepted this offer and chose Pollack, who was greatly respected for his knowledge of the program and its basis in law, to appear before the committee as their spokesman.

The chief complaint of the activists and of Senator McGovern was that the national eligibility standards actually cut some participants from the program. Although the new income standard was a true reform that expanded eligibility in a majority of states, it had the opposite effect in a few others. The most generous AFDC states, particularly California and New York, already had income limits higher than the $360 per month cutoff. An estimated 340,000 recipients would be dropped from the program under the proposed regulations. A related objection was that the new purchase requirements, though they could be no more than 30 percent of income, raised the purchase price slightly for those at the upper end of the income scale. Consequently, some 1.7 million recipients would have their net benefits reduced.

At the Nutrition Committee hearings Pollack raised the issue of deductions as well.[25] In particular, he pressed for a work incentive deduction. Why couldn't food stamps be like AFDC? Also, loans, fellowships, scholarships, and other types of educational grants were counted as part of a family's income, meaning that a food stamp family would have to pay more for stamps if a child received aid to go to school. Why was there no deduction for educational expenses?

In addition to the Nutrition Committee hearings, letters from congressmen exerted pressure on FNS. Representatives and senators sent written comments outlining what they believed congressional intent to be. From the Senate, two letters—one sent by the six Republican members of the Nutrition Committee and the other by twenty Democratic liberals—asserted that USDA had misinterpreted congressional intent in setting an eligibility line that would remove some people from the program. Both letters called for an educational expense deduction and the Democrats pushed for a work disregard.[26]

FNS received six hundred comments on the proposed regulations before the May 17 deadline. Hekman and Springfield felt most vulnerable on the issue of the recipients who would become ineligible in the more generous AFDC states. Lyng and Hardin had no objection to a change, but the Office of Management and Budget (OMB) wanted to keep costs down to what it considered a reasonable level. The extensive criticism from Congress, the press, and the hunger lobby led OMB to relent. In the final regulations the income line remained the same, but eligibility was also granted to anyone who qualified for AFDC. On two much less costly items, the education and work incentive deductions, Springfield and his staff did not feel strongly enough to fight against those favoring these changes. An educational expense deduction and a work disregard for 10 percent of earned income (up to $30 a month) were added to the regulations.

A remaining issue was the increased price of food stamps for recipients at the upper level of the income scale. Springfield and his immediate superiors, Hekman and Lyng, did not oppose a change to bring the prices back to their current level. In a private conversation Lyng told a hunger lobbyist that USDA was ready to back a change but that OMB would not allow it, since revising the schedules for the affected 1.7 million participants would add $200–300 million to the cost of the program. OMB could not be persuaded to permit a revision of the pricing structure. On July 29 the final regulations were published, and they contained no price reductions for the 1.7 million.[27]

Members of the hunger lobby were disheartened by OMB's decision, but they did not give up. Since the new purchase price schedules would not take effect until February 1, 1972, new efforts began around the end of 1971 to get the pricing policy changed. Twenty-eight Republican and Democratic senators wrote a letter to President Nixon's new secretary of agriculture, Earl Butz, complaining about the price regulations. A number of governors met with Butz to ask for his personal intervention. In the Congress bills were introduced to prohibit the new schedules from including a price increase. Finally, Ron Pollack filed a law suit against the regulations.[28]

The administration's resistance to changing the pricing regulation was undercut when the *New York Times* revealed that $202 million in food stamp funds was being impounded.[29] The administration did not feel that it was really impounding the money because it was projecting a lower cost than the amount appropriated. Impoundment was becoming a touchy subject around this time, though, and the administration was not able to refute the story with its own interpretation of what it was doing.[30] Holding back "hunger money" looked bad. The Nutrition Committee promised that it would hold emergency hearings on the impoundment.

On January 16, after a series of meetings among OMB officials, White House aides, representatives of governors, and administrators from Agriculture, Secretary Butz announced that new tables would be constructed to "hold harmless" the price of coupons so that families would not have to pay more than before.[31] The hunger lobby had used all its resources to win a major change in food stamp policy.[32] "It was plain old political pressure," said one high-ranking USDA official. "We couldn't stand the heat."

HOW REGULATIONS ARE WRITTEN: EXPANDING DISCRETION

The rulemaking process underwent some significant changes between 1969 and 1972. Beyond the shift to the more formal notice and comment procedures, notable changes occurred in the way legislators and departmental officials perceived the acceptable limits of administrative discretion. No clear boundaries emerged, though, as administrators were pushed in two different directions. On the one hand, Hardin and his food stamp administrators were asked by critics to expand greatly their notion of acceptable discretionary power, so that the program could be reformed. At the same time, once those officials began to take decisive steps through administrative rules, they found themselves under considerable pressure to share their authority with lobbyists and congressmen.

Why, in one dramatic act, could Hardin claim that USDA had the discretion to revamp the structure of the program totally? He not only ordered a radical revision of the pricing and allocation formulas, but he also committed Congress to a considerably more expensive program. Congress, in fact, had refused on its own to pass a similar reform program. It is true that Hardin was being lobbied strenuously for such reforms and that he had considerable support for them from liberal legislators and, ultimately, from the President of the United States. Still, Hardin moved in defiance of formal congressional intent *not* to reform the program. He disregarded the previously sacrosanct normal purchase requirement in the law and asserted that he had immense discretionary power to redesign the program largely as he wished.

In considering decisions regarding the limits of their discretionary authority, administrators must calculate the risks involved. If they claim expanded discretionary authority, are they likely to succeed without being rebuked by Congress? If they choose not to take action and cite the limitation on their discretion as a reason, will subsequent criticism undermine their status? Another risk that must be taken into account is the possible effect on authority and program control. By claiming wider rulemaking discretion, administrators make a de facto acknowledgment that there is more reason for outsiders to intervene.

As was emphasized in Chapter 1, Davis, Kelley, and Vanneman preferred to have outsiders believe that they did not possess the discretionary power to reform the program. By repeatedly citing the normal purchase requirement, they discouraged potential interveners from believing that lobbying efforts could have some effect. Once they admitted that they had the discretion to make major reforms in the program, legislators like Kennedy or McGovern might intervene repeatedly in the administrative process. The assessment of such risks, however, was judged much differently by Clifford Hardin. For Hardin personally, no real loss of control would accompany expanded discretionary authority. Like any secretary of agriculture, his major concern was with farm policy. Time spent on the food stamp program was time lost from the real priorities of his office. Change in discretionary limits thus became more likely when controversy over food stamps forced the involvement of Hardin.

Although maintaining maximum autonomy over the program was

not of importance to Hardin, potential congressional reaction was. With the public outcry over hunger and with the White House conference approaching, the risks of inaction clearly began to outweigh the displeasure and possible retaliation of conservative congressmen like Poage and Whitten. Once reforms were made through administrative action, the apprehension of Davis and the others was soon borne out. Intervention became more extensive, and program officials found themselves faced with continuing efforts to move them to liberalize the regulations. The incentive to intervene had been increased; USDA could not resist intervention as effectively as it had in the past.

The problem of interpreting congressional intent became increasingly complex between 1969 and 1972. Legislators and interest groups were no longer content to let administrators decide what Congress had meant to say in its statutes. The controversy over legislative intent and administrative discretion was finally stilled by a series of administrative concessions that gave critics almost all the regulatory changes for which they had pressed. Left unresolved, though, were a number of important theoretical questions that arose out of the sustained conflict of this period: Under what general conditions are administrators most likely to take the greatest risks in their interpretation of congressional intent? What factors contribute to informal cooperation between administrators and legislators to reconcile disputes over discretion or intent? Finally, how much discretion should administrators have at their command?

4

CUTTING BACK
ON FOOD STAMPS

THE CONTROVERSY THAT HAD surrounded the food stamp program since 1967 finally began to subside in 1972.. After Secretary of Agriculture Earl Butz made public the administration's decision to rescind the price increase for upper-income recipients, the hunger lobby lost its main issue. Exposés in the press largely disappeared, and the Nutrition Committee held few hearings on issues related to food stamps. The program administrators at the Food and Nutrition Service were able to spend their time on improving the internal management of the program rather than on refuting charges in the *Washington Post*.

If 1972 and 1973 were quiet years for the food stamp program, the period between 1974 and 1976 was just the opposite. The program was once again overtaken by conflicts arising from accusations that food stamp policy was misguided. The protagonists this time were not members of the hunger lobby but conservative politicians. The liberal reforms had made the program highly accessible, and when the economy turned downward during Gerald Ford's term as president, participation in the program leaped upward. Conservatives in Congress and their constituents at home began to believe that it was too easy to get food stamps. For the first time, public opinion turned against the program. Although the program would emerge relatively unscathed from the Ford years and would prosper during Jimmy Carter's presidency, the attack on food stamps would continue with Ronald Reagan in power.

BUREAUCRATIZATION

The food stamp program continued to expand until, in 1975, it was available in all counties in the United States. Fourteen years had passed since the government established the first pilot projects (see Table 2). Finally, though, food stamps became a fully national program, with a single set of eligibility standards and income allotments.

As the program began its expansion into the last nonparticipating areas, FNS grew as well. In the first two years of FNS's existence, the number of food stamp workers increased from around 1,100 to around 1,500.[1] The reorganization of USDA's food distribution services into FNS had proceeded smoothly. In effect, the various food divisions of the Consumer and Marketing Service were simply transferred to the new Food and Nutrition Service. As FNS's first administrator, Edward Hekman was particularly helpful in modernizing the internal management practices of the food stamp bureaucracy.

Two retirements also marked changes in the food stamp program. In 1973 Isabelle Kelley, though only in her fifties, retired so that she could pursue other interests. An older Howard Davis quickly followed Kelley into retirement. After many years of dedicated service, they turned the reins over to a newer group of administrators.

As both the program and FNS expanded, the routinization and bureaucratization of the regulation-writing process increased as well. Regulation writing evolved into a much more specialized task. With FNS, the drafting of regulations came under the authority of the State Agency Operations Branch. In the case of regulations generated by internal review rather than by court order or new legislation, the substance of a proposed regulation is set forth in a position paper by the Operations Group, a handful of staffers who have responsibility over

Table 2. Number of Project Areas with Food Stamp Programs (yearly average)

Fiscal year	Number	Fiscal year	Number
1961	6	1969	1,489
1962	8	1970	1,747
1963	21	1971	2,027
1964	43	1972	2,128
1965	110	1973	2,228
1966	324	1974	2,818
1967	838	1975	3,035
1968	1,027	1976	3,034

NOTE: Most project areas are counties. In a few states, some cities function as separate project areas.

SOURCE: *The Food Stamp Act of 1976*, H. Rept. 1460, 94 Cong., 2 sess., 1976, p. 27.

different aspects of the program. Their position paper, which details the options and alternatives open to FNS, is sent by the head of the State Agency Operations Branch to the director of the Food Stamp Division, who in turn sends it up to the FNS administrator or beyond if the issue is politically sensitive. By that time, an opinion as to the best course of action has been formed within the State Agency Operations Branch, and that view is communicated to the director or administrator as well. Presuming that approval of a policy change is forthcoming—and it usually is—responsibility for the regulation returns to the State Agency Operations Branch. The actual writing of the proposed regulation will fall to someone on the staff of the deputy administrator of this branch.

After a proposed rule is published in the *Federal Register*, the comments received by the Food Stamp Division are reviewed by members of its Program Development Branch. They evaluate the comments, pro and con, and prepare an analysis of the issues raised. Who will make the decision to accept, revise, or reject the regulation in light of the comments depends upon the level of controversy associated with the issue. Most decisions do not reach the assistant secretary for Food and Consumer Services, who has the responsibility for "signing off" on all FNS regulations. No set criteria determine how far up in the organization consultation can be sought on regulations. During the Nixon and Ford years, highly political issues would go to the FNS administrator or, possibly, the assistant secretary of agriculture. After Carter took office, review of all but the most technical regulations began to be centered in the secretary of agriculture's office. Career civil servants in FNS have always sought consultation whenever there has been some doubt about the suitability of a regulation. It seems to be a matter of common sense: Bureaucrats do not want their superiors to be surprised or angered by public criticism of a regulation. There is also an incentive to pass on responsibility for a controversial issue.

As the formal procedures for writing internally generated regulations became more defined and complex, expanded informal procedures for developing statutorily mandated regulations also took hold. During the 1970s administrators from the Food Stamp Division made increasing efforts to consult with the Agriculture Committees on legislation that was being formulated or had recently been passed. Notes taken by food stamp officials at meetings with committee staffers became part of the administrators' understanding of legislative intent. On occasion, these notes have been shown to the counsel's office when a

USDA lawyer has raised questions about the Food Stamp Division's interpretation of congressional intent.

The tendency toward placing more and more administrative guidelines into regulations continued into the mid-1970s. The nineteen pages of regulations that came out of the 1970 legislative amendments grew to forty seven pages in 1975, with no major congressional action in between. In 1975 the courts gave FNS even greater incentive to put its food stamp guidelines into regulations. In *Anderson v. Butz* a federal district court invalidated a food stamp instruction that required rent subsidy payments from a Department of Housing and Urban Development (HUD) program to be counted as part of a food stamp family's income. The court judged the rule invalid because it had not gone through the proper rulemaking procedures.[2] As further protection in the wake of *Anderson*, FNS leaned even more in the direction of putting program rules through the notice and comment process.

FOOD STAMPS UNDER FIRE

A continuing criticism of the food stamp program was that it did not reach enough people. During the 1960s USDA officials had been subjected to charges that millions of eligible, needy individuals were not receiving stamps. In 1974 the criticism took a 180-degree turn. Conservatives began to attack the program repeatedly for supporting too many participants.

The accusations against the food stamp program focused on two fundamental faults. The first complaint was that excessive participation in the program was the result of overly generous eligibility standards. There was much discussion of "high-income" participants— individuals who really did not need help but qualified because of large deductions. For example, a family's eligibility line may have been $400 a month, but, through its deductions, it was qualifying with an actual income of $450 or even $500. The family could deduct high shelter costs and other exclusions like child care or the work disregard *before* its overall income eligibility was determined. A related problem was that a small number of college students was qualifying to receive stamps. This infuriated many taxpayers because it amounted to a back-door scholarship program for middle-class students.

Second, critics charged that the program was the victim of widespread cheating and fraud. The alleged causes of this problem was lax eligibility review of applicants by case workers and a lack of interest on the part of USDA in rooting out ineligibles through "quality control" procedures.

The leading critics of the food stamp program did not, as in the past, come from outside the administration, but from within it. President Ford denounced the program in his 1976 State of the Union address, calling it "scandal riddled." Secretary of Agriculture Butz made no secret of his disdain for the program. Butz did not even feel that his department should administer the program; rather, he thought it should be transferred to HEW (now, Health and Human Services) or some other department. More than any other criticism, however, it was Secretary of the Treasury William Simon's harsh words against the program that proved the most destructive. Speaking before a Junior Achievers Conference in August 1975, Simon described the food stamp program as "spinning out of control" and castigated it as "a well-known haven for chiselers and rip-off artists."[3] Simon's remarks were picked up by the press, and his biting phrases became commonly used catchwords to describe the program.

What happened in such a short period to turn both politicians and public opinion against the program? A number of reasons account for this discontent, but the beginning of the reaction against the program can be traced to the huge increase in participation. In the early years of the program, participation grew slowly as food stamps moved into areas that had commodity programs or no programs at all. Between 1961 and 1964 combined food stamp and commodity participation increased only from 4.5 to 6.5 million individuals. Since participation did not generally increase when a food stamp program replaced a commodity program, most real growth came when projects opened in areas where no previous food aid existed. The largest jump in participation followed the Hardin administrative reforms that made food stamp allotments considerably more generous. Between 1970 (the year the reforms were implemented) and 1971 food stamp participation shot up from 4.3 million to 9.4 million. Some of this growth came from expansion into new areas, but only a tiny fraction of this increase represented former commodity participants. In the next few years program growth stabilized, with combined food stamp and commodity participation growing only slightly (see Table 3).

By the end of 1974, however, the effects of a declining economy began to show up in food stamp participation figures. Between August 1974 and May 1975 unemployment jumped from 5.5 to 8.9 percent of

Table 3. Participation in Family Food Assistance
Programs (monthly average in millions)

Fiscal year	Food stamp	Food distribution	Total[a]
1969	2.9	3.8	6.7
1970	4.3	4.1	8.5
1971	9.4	4.0	13.3
1972	11.1	3.6	14.7
1973	12.2	2.8	15.0
1974	12.9	2.0	14.9
1975	18.9	——[b]	18.9
1976	17.9	——[b]	17.9

[a]Discrepencies in totals and due to rounding errors.
[b]The commodity program had been phased out in all but a few locations by 1975.

SOURCE: USDA figures.

the population. Those who were failing to find work were clearly turning to food stamps. During the same period monthly food stamp participation increased from 15 to 19.4 million individuals. The substantial growth in food stamp participation was paralleled by costs that skyrocketed from $1.5 billion in 1971 to $4.3 billion in 1975. It was not unemployment alone that drove up the cost, but inflation in food prices—18 percent in 1973 alone—as well. Despite the strong relationship between participation and unemployment, conservatives in Congress and in the administration still believed that many undeserving people were being permitted to participate.

A spate of bad publicity about the program also contributed to the negative attitudes that developed toward food stamps. The press, which had been the hunger lobby's most potent resource, now became a powerful weapon in the hands of the opposition. In the fall of 1975 the now defunct *Washington Star* newspaper carried a three-part exposé of the food stamp program. The articles charged that FNS employed such poor methods of verifying applicants' income and was so indifferent to fraud that it was paying out $797 million a year too much in food stamp benefits.[4] A few months earlier, *Reader's Digest*, with its circulation of over 18 million, had published a story that portrayed food stamps as "a program that has literally run amok."[5] *U.S. News and World Report* led into a feature article by stating, "Costs are rising by the billions, abuses are spreading. No wonder there's concern [over] the food-stamp program."[6] Although most of the critical articles about food stamps came from conservative publications and columnists, the wire services occasionally carried neutral accounts of charges by Simon and others.

Possibly the worst piece of publicity came not from a news story but from an advertisement. *Parade* magazine, a supplement to Sunday newspapers around the country, carried a full-page ad informing readers that many of them were unknowingly eligible for food stamps. The ad's headline stated: "Taxpayers Making Up to $16,000 a Year Now Eligible." For only $3.50, a company calling itself the Center for Public Information would send readers a booklet that explained how to qualify for food stamps.[7] The advertisement was an out-and-out fraud. Although program regulations put no actual ceiling on income (because of the system of deductions), there was never any documented case of a family making $16,000 a year being certified eligible for food stamps. Still, for the furor caused by the ad, its claim might as well have been true. *Congressional Quarterly* reported that irate citizens who saw the ad "flooded Congress with their angry letters."[8]

A final reason for the public's changing attitude toward the program had to do with the observations of shoppers in supermarket checkout lines. As more and more unemployed middle-class Americans began to receive food stamps, more and more of their neighbors observed them in the supermarket. When a person pulls out food stamps to pay for his or her purchases, it is all too natural for the next person in line to cast an eye over the types of foods being paid for with the stamps. A steak or other "luxury" item among the selections may incense many observers, who feel that they, the taxpayers, are being taken advantage of. The increasing opportunity to make such random observations at the supermarket generated countless "hamburger and steak" letters to the Congress. Typically, the writer would complain to his congressman that food stamp recipients bought steak, while he himself could afford only hamburger.[9]

These various sources of dissatisfaction with the program cannot be divorced from the manner in which politicians exploited the issue. The misuse, exaggeration, unwarranted extrapolation, and outright distortion of statistics went even beyond the normal range of rhetorical license in political debate. Conservative congressmen did not hesitate to cite the *Parade* ad as evidence of food stamp mismanagement. An assistant secretary of agriculture, Richard Feltner (Richard Lyng's replacement), told the Senate Nutrition Committee that the United States was headed toward a situation in which one-third to one-half of all Americans would be eligible for food stamps. Around the same time,

OMB deleted a section from an FNS study being prepared for the Senate that showed food stamp participation likely to drop.[10]

The cumulative impact of the allegations and exaggerated figures was devastating. By 1976 the image of food stamps was indeed that of a program "run amok" and beset by scandal. An extremely high level of participation in the program was an irrefutable fact; the causes of this level of participation remained a subject of dispute between liberals and conservatives.[11]

CUTTING BACK THROUGH REGULATION

The real and exaggerated problems of the food stamp program rendered it politically vulnerable. Despite the efforts of the Senate Nutrition Committee and of pro–food stamp groups to give some perspective to the participation figures, the perception spread that there was something severely awry with the program. Even if the high level of participation could be accounted for by the unemployment rate, nothing could explain away the errors that led to millions of dollars in overpayments. It became inevitable that efforts would be made to cut back on the food stamp program.

The first try at conservative reform of the program came in late 1974. On November 18 President Ford announced a sweeping plan to reduce federal spending. By cutting the budget, Ford hoped to curb the inflationary spiral that was weakening the economy. The over all proposed budget cut was $4.6 billion, and a large portion of the savings was to come from the food stamp program: $215 million in the remainder of fiscal year 1975 and $650 million annually thereafter. The cutback in food stamp spending was to be implemented through regulation.

The Ford plan was based on new purchase price schedules that would have instituted a uniform price for food stamps at 30 percent of a family's net income. The 30 percent ceiling, established by law in 1970, was a reflection of the administrative reforms put into effect the year before by Clifford Hardin. Hardin, of course, had lowered purchase prices even below 30 percent. The average food stamp family paid 23 percent of its income for stamps under the Hardin tables. By requiring all families to pay 30 percent for their stamps (except those so poor that they got their stamps for free), the government could save an enormous amount of money. The savings would have actually been much greater than the $650 million that the Ford administration projected. For many families, the extra charge for stamps would cut their bonus so much as to make participation no longer worthwhile. Liberals charged that there would be at least a 10 percent dropout rate and that actual savings would be closer to a billion dollars a year.[12] Ninety-five percent of all food stamp recipients would be affected by the new pricing formulas.

The origins of the proposed changes go back to a directive from OMB to USDA to reduce its spending by over $500 million as part of the upcoming government-wide budget cutback. Although it was up to Butz to decide where the cuts would be made, it was a foregone conclusion that they would come chiefly out of FNS.[13] Butz had always felt that true agricultural programs were inadequately funded because USDA's total budget was so inflated by the inclusion of food stamp expenditures.

Aside from its political problems, the food stamp program was in a precarious position because the cuts apparently could be accomplished through rgulation. In the words of one FNS official, "The thing about this was that it could be done very fast. You just publish new tables and there's nothing else." Using food stamp regulations to cut expenditures meant that Congress, always hesitant to take benefits away from constituents, would not have to be involved. After FNS "carefully reviewed and analyzed" 4,317 comments (almost all of them negative) on their proposed regulations,[14] the new tables were published in final form on January 22, 1975.[15] The regulations were scheduled to take effect on March 1.

Constituency pressure to stop the cuts never really had to be exerted on Congress: It was anticipated. Congress reacted rapidly to block the new regulations, largely for the reason that fixing the purchase price at 30 percent would have the most adverse impact on one- and two-person families. This was a strategic error, because one- and two-person households are composed disproportionately of elderly persons. In dollars and cents, the price increases were quite drastic for the smallest families. A single person with an income of $150 a month, who was paying $33 for $46 worth of stamps, would have his purchase price raised to $45. Obviously no one would bother to participate for a single bonus dollar of stamps. The *New York Times* editorialized that the new schedules looked like they had been "designed by Marie Antoinette."[16]

The issue quickly became one of cutting back aid to the elderly rather than one of controlling an exploding and abused program. Bills to rescind the regulations appeared as soon as the newly elected Congress convened. On February 4 the full House passed a bill, 374–38, to stop the regulations. A day later the Senate approved the same bill by an equally lopsided 76–8 vote. President Ford allowed the bill to become law without his signature.[17] The legislation prohibited any increases in the purchase price for the remainder of the calendar year. To ensure that the bill would be passed fast enough to stop the regulations, no attempt was made by either house to legislate any substantive reforms of the program.

It is highly unusual for the Congress to react immediately to regulations by passing a law to stop their implementation. What is even more unusual about Congress's action in this case is that the regulations were aimed at trimming a program popularly perceived to be too big and too loosely administered. Clearly, what killed the reforms was the effect the schedules would have on the elderly. Also, the economic recession deepened significantly between October 1974, when the cuts were first conceived, and January 1975, when Congress came back into session. Unemployment jumped about two full percentage points during this short time. Furthermore, the congressional move to stop the regulations preceded the most destructive publicity about the program: The Simon speech and the *Parade* ad were yet to come. Finally, there was a sense in the Congress that it was going to pass reform legislation soon and that it should be Congress, and not the administration, that should decide on program changes.

The administration had calculated badly, and the effort resulted in an embarrassing legislative defeat. Only forty Republicans in both houses had voted in support of the president. Ford's supporters in USDA contended that they did not know that the new tables would hurt the elderly so badly. Staff social scientists in FNS refused to be scapegoats as well, claiming that they gave adequate forewarning of the practical effect of the regulations.[18] The administration, however, was not yet ready to give up on using regulations to reform the food stamp program.

A SECOND TRY

The Ford administration's decision to try again to reform the program through regulation is inextricably tied to Congress's efforts to pass a food stamp bill. In 1975 and 1976 everyone acknowledged that the food stamp program needed overhauling, but there was little agreement on the specifics of reform. Generally, for conservatives, reform meant a sharp cutback in the income eligibility line, tighter accountability controls for recipients, a more effective work registration requirement, and elimination of students and striking workers from the program. For many liberals, despite the growing public disenchantment with the program, reform meant abolishing the purchase price for all participants.

After Congress's defeat of the Ford regulations in February 1975, the administration once again took the initiative. FNS staffers worked quickly to produce analyses of various issues and potential policy changes for Secretary Butz, who sent a package of administrative reforms to the president on May 31. The secretary, however, deferred to the White House on the most important policy change of all: How many people should be cut from the program? Ford turned the matter over to his Domestic Council for a recommendation. A dispute then developed as to who would control the food stamp policy recommendations. OMB—particularly, Deputy Director Paul O'Neill—wanted an administration position in favor of a major cutback in the number of persons eligible for food stamps. Representative Robert Michel (R.–Ill.), a long-time friend of Gerald Ford during their years in the House together, was pushing the president to back his own conservative bill. On the Domestic Council, Arthur Quern, a young presidential aide who had come to Washington with Vice President Nelson Rockefeller, found himself unable to glue these conservative views to the more moderate ones from the White House.[19] The president decided initially to side with the Domestic Council and withheld any major recommendations to the Congress pending further review.[20] The administration had lost the initiative, and liberals and conservatives in both houses moved ahead with their own legislation.

The conservative attempt to legislate reform centered on a bill sponsored by Representative Michel and Senator James Buckley (R., Cons.–N.Y.). Although the Buckley-Michel bill was much too extreme to stand a chance of passage, it had 120 cosponsors and represented the conservatives' main bargaining chip in any attempts at compromise. Drafted by David Swoap, a former welfare official for Governor Ronald Reagan of California, the Buckley-Michel bill was designed to cut costs by roughly $2 billion a year—approximately 40 percent of all food stamp expenditures. This extensive cost reduction was to be achieved by lowering the effective eligibility line by almost $1,000 in yearly income for an average family.

The liberal forces in Congress coalesced behind a bill introduced by Robert Dole (R.–Kan.) and George McGovern. The chief feature of the Dole-McGovern bill was the elimination of the purchase requirement, the last great barrier to participation.[21] Instead of purchasing their stamps, individuals would receive for free the amount of bonus coupons due to them according to their income level on the sliding scale. The proposed income eligibility line was also considerably more generous than that in the Buckley-Michel bill. Dole's sponsorship of this liberal measure was something of a surprise, given his usual midwestern Republican conservatism. From his work on both the Agriculture and the Nutrition committees, however, he had come to realize that the purchase price was a major problem for many potential participants.[22]

The missing piece of legislation was the administration's bill. Prior to finally releasing it, Quern met privately with Michel and Hyde Murray, senior Republican staffer on the House Agriculture Committee. When Michel and Murray saw the particulars of the bill, they were incensed. In their opinion the bill was far too moderate, and they told Quern that the bill was unacceptable to congressional Republicans. Later Murray, who had worked for years with Ford in the House, met privately with the president to tell him personally how bad the bill was. Ford withheld the legislation, and, again, it was back to the drawing board for Quern.[23] Quern's instructions were to produce a more conservative bill, and in October, after months of delay, the much-revised Ford administration bill was ready. Using an eligibility line between those of the Buckley-Michel and Dole-McGovern bills, the Ford bill would have forced an estimated 20–30 percent of current participants off the food stamp rolls. Nevertheless, the bill still did not go as far as Michel wanted. After agreeing to give the bill a courtesy introduction, Michel, along with David Swoap, took scissors and tape to the bill and added eleven provisions of their own. When a newspaper reporter asked about the discrepency between the Senate version of the Ford bill and the revised House version, Michel replied, "I know what the President wants."[24]

All the negotiating over the president's bill notwithstanding, the Congress continued to pull in two opposite directions, and the administration's bill failed as a bridge for liberal and conservative compromise. Late in 1975 the Senate began to move toward eventual passage of a bill that would not entail any significant cutback in the program. The liberals traded deletion of a no purchase price provision for Agriculture Committee Chairman Herman Talmadge's (D.–Ga.) support for a relatively unchanged eligibility line.

The Ford White House continued a perfunctory backing of its bill through the latter part of 1975. Early into the new year, however, Ford and his aides decided to give up on the Congress and to try reform through regulatory action once again. There were two reasons for this choice. First was the Senate bill, with its liberal income eligibility line. As one White House aide commented, "We realized that in terms of what they were likely to do, it wasn't going to save any money, [and] it might even cost us." The second reason had to do with the president's political problems. In February he would face conservative challenger Ronald Reagan in the New Hampshire presidential primary, and Reagan was already making welfare abuse one of his major campaign issues. Reagan told audience after audience the story of the "welfare queen," a Chicago woman who bilked the government out of $150,000 a year in fraudulent welfare payments.

The decision to put the provisions of the Ford bill into effect through administrative regulation came at a January meeting of Ford, Butz, USDA Undersecretary Jack Knebal, OMB head James Lynn, and Art Quern and James Cannon of the Domestic Council. Ford asked OMB to review this plan, and by mid-February he was ready to act. Ford's directive was relayed to John Harris and Merwin Kaye, two lawyers in the USDA's general counsel's office, who were told, "Do as much as you can through regulation." The two lawyers were familiar with the program, but their usual role was to clear regulations, not to write them. They did their best, converting as much of the administration's bill as they could into administrative regulations.

The White House announced its intention to reform the program through regulation on February 20, just four days before the New Hampshire primary. The White House regulations set a general price for stamps at 30 percent of income, but the tables were drawn in such a way as to reduce the adverse impact on one- and two-person households. The regulations also outlined a tough work registration requirement, replaced the system of itemized deductions with one standard deduction for all families, and stipulated that eligibility be based on a family's income of the previous ninety days, rather than on current and anticipated income. The comments received were almost all critical, but the proposed regulations were still relatively unchanged when published in final form on May 7.[25]

For the career civil servants in the FNS, the Ford regulations were one more humiliation. After the indignity of the Simon attack, the *Parade* ad, and all the other unfortunate publicity the program had received, it was a final insult to be completely removed from food stamp policy making. They had no substantive input on the regulations at all. "When the regs came through here, we had forty-eight hours to clean them up," said one FNS official bitterly.

Although the public, which had been angered by stories of program abuses, generally supported the second set of Ford regulations, the hunger lobby was outraged anew. "It wasn't a matter of whether we would be sued, but when," said one FNS administrator. And sued they were. The Food Research and Action Center (FRAC), representing seventy food stamp families, as well as states, church groups, civil rights organizations, and labor unions, filed suit a few days after the regulations became final. FRAC first won a temporary restraining order, and then, on June 18, it obtained a preliminary injunction. Federal District Judge John Lewis Smith ruled that the government had exceeded its authority in issuing the regulations.[26] Although the Ford administration vowed to appeal, the regulations were effectively dead for the remainder of the year. If the Democrats could beat Gerald Ford in November, the regulations would become moot.

For the second time in two years the Ford administration had tried and failed to reform the food stamp program through regulations. Nor was the Congress anymore successful in reforming the program. After months of quarreling, the House Agriculture Committee finally produced a bill during the summer of 1976. A compromise that nobody really liked, it died in the Rules Committee. The word around Capitol Hill was that congressmen did not want to vote on food stamp legislation. It was an election year, and no matter how they acted, they would anger some voters. After all that had transpired between 1974 and 1976, the program had been left unchanged.

THE HUNGER LOBBY

At the same time that conservatives were trying to cut back the food stamp program, the hunger lobby actively sought to protect and expand the rights of food stamp recipients. The hunger lobby had changed much since it began to be a major influence in the late 1960s. As public opinion and media coverage became less favorable, the hunger lobby began to rely more on litigation, a method of lobbying that is obviously less dependent on public support. Two of the newer organizations, the Community Nutrition Institute (CNI) and the Food Research and Action Center, came to dominate the loose coalition of pro–food stamp advocates.

Transition in the hunger lobby occurred in personnel as well as in organization. As individuals like Marian Wright, Robert Choate, and Edgar Cahn left to work on different social issues, other activists took their places. Together with Ron Pollack of FRAC, Robert Greenstein of CNI and Arnold Mayer of the Amalgamated Meat Cutters Union emerged as the chief strategists and lobbyists for those in favor of a liberal, highly accessible program.

Arnold Mayer, the chief Washington representative of the Meat Cutters Union, became active on food stamps because the union leadership felt a social obligation to work on behalf of those who could not afford to eat well on their own. Although theoretically there might be some benefit to meatcutters from the food stamp program, it would be too insignificant to provide a major incentive for the union's involvement. Mayer chiefly aided the hunger coalition by directing legislative lobbying.

Robert Greenstein came to CNI after leaving graduate school in history at the University of California. Although he had no practical background for his job at CNI, Rod Leonard hired him anyway, and Greenstein quickly became one of the leading experts on the food stamp program. Leonard also provided the hunger lobby with a communications link by establishing the *CNI Weekly Report* (later renamed *Nutrition Week*). This eight-page newsletter covers all governmental feeding programs and serves as an invaluable asset to anyone interested in influencing legislative and administrative policy. Newsletter subscriptions are a central source of funding for CNI. The size of CNI's staff has fluctuated with the rise and fall of federal grant money; close to thirty men and women were working for the group at the end of the Carter years.

Ron Pollack was able to start the Food Research and Action Center when the government's Office of Economic Opportunity asked him to organize a conference to educate legal service lawyers on what they could do to help the poor with federal feeding programs. Pollack told them that he had an idea for a more effective way to spend that money. Until the Reagan administration came into office, FRAC received most of its financial support from the government. With a staff that grew as large as twenty-six in 1980, FRAC has been the backbone of the hunger lobby, involved in an advisory or primary capacity in almost all major food stamp litigation.

Many other civil rights, church, union, and poverty organizations are sympathetic to the food stamp program and participate to a limited degree in the advocacy work of the hunger lobby. It is usually the case in Washington politics that a few organizations take the lead in the lobbying efforts of a much larger coalition. In 1975, for example, a coalition of sixty to seventy groups began meeting to discuss strategy on the food stamp legislation being considered by the Congress. Nevertheless, it was Mayer, Greenstein, and Pollack who were making the decisions. As a representative of a church group complained, "What they'd do is first have a small meeting to discuss what to do, and then they'd have a larger meeting the next day to bring in the rest of us." It was an oligarchy of convenience, though, as the other organizations were able or willing to devote only limited resources to food stamp lobbying.

Although the antihunger forces fought hard for an acceptable food stamp bill from the Ninety-fourth Congress, they were not displeased when the Congress failed to act. Given the mood of the country, they much preferred to take the chance that a better bill might emerge after public anger about the program subsided and, possibly, after a Democrat replaced President Ford. During this time the hunger lobby nevertheless made some important gains for food stamp recipients through FRAC's litigation. It was FRAC's suit, of course, that stopped the second set of Ford administration regulations. FRAC was also extremely effective in forcing USDA to change program regulations to make food stamps more accessible and to ensure procedural rights for food stamp recipients. Some of the cases that FRAC won included a ruling that prohibited counties from voluntarily withdrawing from the program and obtained reimbursement for food stamp participants wrongly denied benefits. In another important case, FRAC was party to a suit that forced USDA to comply with the law by taking positive action to locate and educate eligible nonparticipants.[27] Against the professed desires of Earl Butz, USDA began outreach programs to find more nonparticipants.[28]

FRAC became so successful in its litigation that other food stamp activists began to expect that the group would win any time it filed a suit. The basis of FRAC's success during these years was Pollack's exceptional understanding of how the program worked. When asked about Pollack, a lawyer in the USDA counsel's office replied, "His knowledge of the program is superior to that of anyone here." The key to Pollack's strategy was his ability to translate questions of law into graphic, human terms. When filing a court suit, he used only plaintiffs whose situations would become so desperate if the court did not rule in their favor that a judge could not help but think that the regulation under question was arbitrary or irrational.

The only person outside of government whose knowledge of program operations matched Pollack's was Robert Greenstein of CNI. Greenstein was a major resource for congressmen who favored liberal reform and was in fact more valuable to them than many of the staffers who worked for the Nutrition and Agriculture committees. At a time when the program was quite unpopular, Pollack, Greenstein, and members of their organizations provided immeasurable service to the millions of Americans in the food stamp program. They acted for food stamp recipients, but not at their instigation. No food stamp recipients actually belong to CNI or FRAC.

PEACE . . .

The food stamp program never became a major issue during the presidential election of 1976. Despite all the controversy that had surrounded the two sets of Ford administration regulations, campaign promises about the operation of the food stamp program were unlikely to sway voters one way or another. Still, for liberal backers of the program, Jimmy Carter, or any other Democrat, was clearly preferable to Gerald Ford.

Thus, Carter's election was a relief for antihunger advocates, who knew the program was at least safe from drastic cutbacks. Although Carter's position on the question of liberal reform of the program was something of a mystery, an indicator was soon provided with the appointment of Bob Bergland to the post of secretary of agriculture. From the viewpoint of food stamp supporters, the three-term representative and former farmer from Minnesota was an excellent choice. A president's first priority in selecting a secretary of agriculture is to choose someone respected by farmers. In Bergland, Carter found someone highly regarded by the hunger lobby as well. On the House Agriculture Committee, Bergland had been a staunch supporter of the program, and his office had even been used as a meeting place for the liberal legislative coalition working on behalf of the program. Bergland supported the elimination of the purchase price, and his appointment meant this reform stood a good chance of passage.

When Bergland made his appointments to fill USDA policy positions, his choices in the food stamp area could not have been more pleasing to liberals. Bob Greenstein of CNI was chosen as an aide to Bergland for food assistance programs. Another public interest lobbyist, Carol Tucker Foreman of the Consumer Federation of America, was named as assistant secretary for Food and Consumer Services to replace Richard Feltner. In the Food and Nutrition Service, two more public interest activists, Lewis Straus and Christine Van Lenten, became FNS administrator and director of legislative affairs, respectively. Both Straus and Van Lenten had been working in the New Jersey-based National Child Nutrition Project.

Bergland's appointments marked a striking shift in the administration of the food stamp program. The four top political appointees were all former public interest lobbyists. After years of hostile treatment from USDA, public interest groups were now on the inside running the program.[29]

The Ninety-fifth Congress took up food stamp legislation almost immediately because an omnibus farm bill was needed within the year. That food stamp legislation could be considered along with a farm bill, unlike the situation in 1975–1976, was a distinct advantage to program supporters. Logrolls with farm state congressmen could be used, and enactment of the legislation came quickly and without much conflict. President Carter's proposal included elimination of the purchase price, and it was soon apparent that enough votes were there to pass it. House Agriculture Committee Chairman Thomas Foley favored this change, although his Senate counterpart, Herman Talmadge, refused to go along, declaring, "Free food stamps is not reform of the program, it is destruction of the program."[30] Talmadge's outburst was the dying gasp of the original "help the poor help themselves" concept behind the program.

With the farm state members of the Agriculture Committees in a conciliatory mood, and with the administration backing the proposal fully, abolition of the purchase price emerged as the cornerstone of the food stamp bill passed in September 1977.[31] Recipients now simply receive the amount of coupons that corresponds to the difference between the standard allotment and the old purchase price. Other significant changes involved a reduction in the eligibility line,[32] a change in the method of calculating deductions, and the mandating of "workfare" pilot projects. In addition to a sixty-dollar per month standard deduction for all families, an additional deduction of as much as seventy-five dollars was allowed for combined shelter and child care costs. The workfare section of the bill specified that fourteen experimental projects be started to test the effect of a stringent work requirement on program participation. Recipients in workfare projects are required to take a government-sponsored job, for which they are paid in food stamps. In essence, participants work for what all other recipients receive for free.

Carter appointees changed the process of writing food stamp regulations significantly. Soon after the law was passed, public hearings were held in seventeen locations around the country. At least one official from the Food and Nutrition Service in Washington attended each hearing, along with regional FNS administrators, to hear recipients talk about their problems with the program. Although the public meetings, as one FNS official acknowledged, "were not a generator of new ideas," food stamp administrators were generally pleased with their attempt to make citizen participation part of the regulatory process.

Drafting the regulations mandated by the new legislation became the job of an ad hoc task force headed by Alberta Frost and Susan McAndrew, the two individuals who were normally in charge of regulation writing. However, the existing procedures and personnel were not capable of dealing with the massive job of writing hundreds of pages of regulations and explanatory text. Frost's core group of a half dozen or so created thirty or so smaller subgroups on individual issues that drew on staff from all areas of FNS. After the subgroups completed drafts of options and regulatory language, the task force reworked them and then sent them up for review. According to the line charts, the paper flow went from the Frost task force to Food Stamp Division head Nancy Snyder, to Christine Van Lenten, to Lewis Straus, to Carol Foreman, and finally to Bob Greenstein. In practice, Van Lenten and Greenstein handled the real review. These two maintained a firm control over the content of the regulations and sent many back for revisions. Although the former public interest lobbyists generally worked well with the career civil servants, neither group felt entirely positive about the other. One high-ranking careerist said of herself and her colleagues, "A lot of people feel that the administrators are looking upon them . . . with mistrust; that they don't operate with the full confidence of these individuals." The civil servants believed they were viewed as sinners for being "good soldiers" when they carried out the Ford administration's regulations.

The new administrators of the program did not forget their origins: public interest groups were given unusual access to USDA and FNS decision makers. Early in the development of the regulations, FRAC lobbyists held a two-day meeting with key administrators. Drafts of regulations were frequently sent to FRAC and occasionally to other groups for comment before they were readied for issuance in notice form. Indeed, public interest groups enjoyed such ready access that state welfare administrators began to resent them. One FNS official noted, "The feedback from the states is that FNS is being only responsive to FRAC and CNI and ignoring their concerns. They complain that FRAC has things before they do and that CNI knows policy before they get it."

The final regulations took much longer than expected to complete, owing to underestimation of the complexity of the project and unrealistic timetables. Seven and one-half months after the passage of the bill, the first batch of regulations (eighty pages of program rules and explanatory material) was issued for public comment.[33] Not surprisingly, the public interest groups pronounced themselves quite pleased with the package. For their part, members of Congress had little to say. Conservatives recognized that the liberals had total control over the program and made little effort to influence the regulations. The liberals themselves had full confidence in the program's administrators and saw no real reason to intervene in rulemaking.

In the life of the food stamp program the Carter presidency marked four years of relative quiet, with the program free of many of the conflicts that had enervated it in the past. It was a time when the program's most persistent critics were given responsibility for it. Most important, this period witnessed the resolution of the most vexing problem the program had faced since its inception. From the very first pilot projects, some of the individuals who needed the program most had found the purchase price an obstacle to participation. After sixteen years, welfare in the form of food coupons was finally free.

. . . AND WAR

With the election of Ronald Reagan, the food stamp program once again became the target of a hostile president. Over the course of many election campaigns, Reagan had stressed that welfare was too easy to obtain and that the government needed stricter eligibility criteria. Equally disastrous for program supporters in 1980 was the Republican party's sweep in the Senate and its gains in the House. Jesse Helms (R.–N.C.), a virulent critic of the program, became chairman of the Senate Agriculture Committee. George McGovern, long-time champion of the program, lost his Senate seat. Helms sounded the battle cry of the new guard when he proclaimed that he wanted to get rid of the "parasites who have infested the food stamp program."[34]

After the election, Ronald Reagan appointed John Block, an Illinois farmer and state administrator, to be his secretary of agriculture. Block had little interest in food stamps, and it soon became clear that major decisions about the program would be made at the White House and at OMB. When Reagan proposed his sweeping budget reductions in February 1981, the food stamp program was singled out for one of the largest cuts — $1.8 billion for fiscal year 1982. The president deftly defused charges of harshness toward the poor by declaring that a "safety net" of programs left largely untouched would provide for the "truly needy."

The hunger lobby moved swiftly to try to protect the program, but none of the liberal activists believed that food stamps could come through the budgetary process unscathed. The question was how much the program would ultimately be cut, not whether it would be cut. Bob Greenstein, who became head of an antihunger group called the Project on Food Assistance and Poverty after leaving USDA, coordinated the lobbying along with Arnold Mayer and staffers from FRAC and CNI. The food stamp advocates lost a crucial early vote in the Senate Budget Committee when the Republicans rejected a more moderate cut on a party-line vote. Thereafter, it was evident that President Reagan would achieve most of the food stamp cuts he wanted. The best the hunger lobbyists could do was to help defeat proposals by Senator Helms and others for more extreme cuts.

Major changes enacted under the sweeping budget cuts included: a less timely indexing of benefits to the rate of inflation (savings for fiscal year 1982: $518 million); a restriction of first-month benefits to a prorated amount corresponding to the days left in the month ($495 million); elimination of all households with gross incomes above 130 percent of the poverty line ($110 million); more stringent standard and shelter deductions ($237 million); a lower earned income deduction ($48 million); conversion of the program in Puerto Rico into a block grant ($70 million); and a prohibition against striker and boarder eligibility ($50 million each). Overall, these and other cuts reduced food stamp expenditures by an estimated $1.65 billion for fiscal year 1982 and by a projected $6 billion between 1982 and 1984.[35]

The Reagan philosophy toward welfare is most clearly embodied in those changes directed at the working poor. Throughout his political career, Reagan has held that welfare ought to be targeted toward those at the very bottom of the income ladder. For the poor who have some income from a job, welfare is a possible disincentive for increased work effort. From the Reagan point of view, then, the lower earned income deduction and the elimination of so-called high-income families would make individuals work harder because they would have less of a cushion to support them.[36] Still, no real attempt was made to target benefits to the neediest individuals. The nonworking poor also came out worse under the Reagan plan than before because of other cuts.

The scope and depth of the food stamp cuts stunned many program supporters. In retrospect, the program was more vulnerable than many people had realized. The program's most significant problem now is that public opinion has turned against it. A Gallup Poll (for *Newsweek*) taken in February 1981 revealed that 61 percent of the sample thought the government was spending too much for food stamps, and the program proved to be the most unpopular among the ten that respondents were asked to evaluate. Other polls confirm the public's dislike of the food stamp program.[37]

Why has this program, which enjoyed strong public support for so many years, fallen out of favor with the American people? In large part, it is because the program itself has become the issue instead of hunger in America. Ironically, the food stamp program suffers because it has been a success. Together with child nutrition programs, it has eliminated widespread hunger and malnutrition.[38] The public perceives that hunger is no longer a serious problem in America. Consequently, discussion of the food stamp program has focused on issues such as eligibility and fraud.

Over the years, political rhetoric and misleading publicity have taken their toll. Still, the politicians are responding to the feelings of constituents, and many of those constituents see and resent the individuals at their supermarkets who buy groceries with food stamps. With participation up to 22 million a month, there are more and more shoppers to observe, many of whom may seem no different than any other shopper in dress or manner, which can lead to questions about eligibility standards. As long-time program advocate John Kramer put it, "Everytime you see someone in the checkout line using food stamps, and you're not, you've been lobbied against the program. It's out in the open in every supermarket every day."[39]

The cuts in funds for food stamps were also facilitated by separating the program from the farm bill. The Reagan administration focused its attack on domestic programs by pressing for cuts in the funding ceilings set by the House and Senate Budget Committees. Reagan was the first president to use this relatively new process, created as part of the Budget and Impoundment Control Act of 1974, to restrain federal spending. The tactic prevented urban liberals from using a logroll with farm state congressmen to protect the program. Although an effort at logrolling may emerge in subsequent sessions of Congress, the options of program supporters are now severely limited during Budget Committee deliberations.

With the Reagan administration in power, food stamp advocates are back in their familiar role of outsiders looking in. FNS has excluded hunger lobby representatives from the rulemaking process. When an FNS task force was created to examine food stamp regulations and propose changes, no client advocates were permitted to participate. Arvid Dopson, who headed the task force, responded to questions about this decision by saying that the meetings are "basically not open. I'm not sure [a client or advocate] could be a contributor."[40]

HOW REGULATIONS ARE WRITTEN: INTEREST GROUPS AND PUBLIC OPINION

The role of the hunger lobby has grown over time with the food stamp program. Early in the program's life, there was virtually no interest group activity. Between 1961 and the middle of 1967, policy initiation came from bureaucrats and elected officials. After the Kennedy-Clark trip to Mississippi, citizen groups began to function in an agenda-setting capacity. The work of some of the early groups was instrumental in making Americans aware of the severe hunger problem and in promoting food stamps as a political issue. These groups, like the National Council on Hunger and Malnutrition and the Poor People's Campaign, proved less successful at more traditional forms of lobbying with the Congress and USDA.

Only after Richard Nixon came to office did food stamp groups begin to act as consistent and effective legislative and administrative lobbies. Working with their allies in the press and on the Senate Nutrition Committee, FRAC and CNI established themselves as major forces in the rulemaking process between 1971 and 1976. During the Carter years, the hunger groups were welcomed into the administrative process. FRAC and CNI enjoyed almost unlimited access to USDA officials and worked closely with administrators to formulate program regulations. Ronald Reagan's election put an end to this arrangement, but it has not diminished the hunger lobby's determination to fight for the program.

If this were a study of an economic regulatory agency and one of its programs, it would hardly seem surprising that strong interest groups emerged to protect relevant constituencies. It is to be expected that economic interests will be represented in Washington. The same expectation does not hold for clients of social service and welfare programs. It is a truism of American politics that the poor are difficult to organize and not well represented in Washington.[41] In the case of the food stamp program, however, active representation of client interests continues. The poor themselves are not organized, of course, but two well-staffed public interest lobbies act on their behalf. Through their superior knowledge of the program, their willingness to litigate, their ability to publicize departmental actions, and their sheer persistence, these two lobbies have had a far-reaching impact on USDA policy making. Unlike the early years of the program, the poor now have a voice in Washington.

The hunger lobby remains frustrated, however, in developing an ongoing relationship with USDA that would make it a partner in food stamp rulemaking. More often than not, program officials have been hostile toward food stamp lobbyists. Conservative administrators see little to be gained from dealing with their critics. Unlike business trade associations, which are usually able at least to discuss policy problems with both Democratic and Republican administrators, welfare groups have had limited access to Republicans in power.

Food stamp policy makers have been influenced not only by lobbying groups but also by public opinion. When hunger became an issue, strong public support for feeding programs left officials little choice but to move in the direction of liberalizing and expanding the program. By the time Gerald Ford became president, hunger had ceased to be an issue, and the "welfare mess" was disturbing many Americans. When Ronald Reagan succeeded Jimmy Carter, widespread public opinion supported cutbacks on food stamps, now one of the government's most unpopular programs.

Public opinion has always acted as a general constraint on the program, facilitating administrators' and politicians' efforts aimed at its growth or contraction. Presidential elections have served as the most important link between popular opinion and policy making in Washington. John Kennedy made hunger at least a minor issue in the 1960 election, and his victory gave life to the program. Whatever his humanitarian instinct, Richard Nixon could not help but be swayed by the public's perception of widespread hunger and malnutrition. The Hardin reforms were in no small part the result of public outcry over the problem. Likewise, the disappearance of hunger as an issue and the rising concern over welfare and the budget led to the Ford and Reagan attacks on food stamps.

Yet, although presidential elections have linked public opinion to policy making, they have done so in an imprecise way. Jimmy Carter pushed Congress to enact a major liberalization of the program in spite of waning public support for food stamps. Presidential elections can never be a perfect barometer for public sentiment about the program because food stamps will never be a central, decisive issue in presidential elections. With an issue of secondary importance in races for the White House, there is potential for a "mismatch" of public opinion and presidential purpose. The 1976 election was just such a case.

But if the system has worked imperfectly, one must still conclude that the public at large has been heard at the administrative level. The ideological concerns of the president, the intervention of congressmen, and the general contours of public opinion are all considerations that are taken into account by agency administrators. When one segment of public opinion is allowed to prevail over others, it can usually be justified by presidential elections that provide each president with his "mandate." Yet no election results can justify the wholesale exclusion of client representatives from the rulemaking process. Elections should make a difference in policy, but a rulemaking process that ensures some form of citizen involvement should exist in all administrations.

PART 2

REGULATIONS, SOCIAL POLICY, AND THE POLITICAL PROCESS

5

CONGRESSIONAL INVOLVEMENT IN ADMINISTRATIVE RULEMAKING

THROUGHOUT THE HISTORY OF the food stamp program, legislators have tried to shape or change administrative regulations. As noted at the outset of this study, congressmen exert such influence by writing or rewriting legislation, by intervening in the rulemaking process itself, or (in years past) by using the legislative veto. These are the means by which Congress asserts its legislative prerogatives to determine the course of public policy. Administrators, in turn, must anticipate how Congress will react to the different regulatory options they consider. Ultimately, then, the degree of legislative control over food stamps or any other domestic program is directly related to Congress's propensity to intervene while regulations are being written and its willingness to review agency regulations rigorously.

LEGISLATIVE RESPONSE TO ADMINISTRATIVE REGULATION

What happens after a bill becomes a law and after the regulations following from that bill are written? The interaction between legislators and administrators is continuous, but what may be thought of as a "legislative response" is a decision point within an ongoing process. These decision points represent important stages in legislative policy making because they offer Congress opportunities to reflect upon its own failures in writing earlier legislation. They also provide a chance to increase legislative control by rewriting administrative regulations. Congress is often accused of creating programs with broad guidelines and then letting agencies develop the substantive policy that must be made.[1] Even if this is true at the beginning of an agency's or a program's life, the neglect will not necessarily continue. Administrative regulations force Congress into decisions or "nondecisions" regarding the extent and detail of its involvement in all areas of program policy making.

The four types of legislative responses to be presented below describe a range of activity that is brought about by the issuance of regulations. The factors that determine these various forms of congressional reaction to regulations include the degree of internal legislative agreement, the opportunities available for changing administrative decisions, and the intensity of feeling by those desiring specific policies. By considering these various response patterns, we may learn more about how Congress chooses to modify or concur with administrative regulations.

Goal affirmation is essentially a positive response on the part of Congress to action taken by administrators. It usually takes place where consensus dominates or where an intense minority is able to prevail over an apathetic majority. The clearest example of goal affirmation is when regulations are put into statute. Administrators make policy decisions largely independent of congressional directive, and Congress later adopts these policies through statute as its own.

The Food Stamp Act of 1964, the original authorizing legislation, is a case of goal affirmation. Although a dispute occurred in the Congress over whether or not the government should create such a program, there was little debate over what the program should look like.[2] Instead, Congress generally adopted the program guidelines designed by USDA administrators Howard Davis, Isabelle Kelley, and Sam Vanneman for the pilot projects run by the department. The critical policy decisions contained in these pilot project guidelines were adopted wholesale in the language of the ensuing law.

An intermediate step prior to goal affirmation through statute is informal legislative clearance of administrative policy before the issuance of a regulation. Key committee chairmen can be consulted, as happened in 1969, when Secretary of Agriculture Clifford Hardin moved to lower the purchase price and raise the food stamp benefits. Hardin was proposing a set of regulatory reforms that the House had been unwilling to pass as legislation. He briefed W. R. Poage and Jamie Whitten as to his intentions. Though opposed to liberalizing the program, the two congressmen decided not to challenge Hardin. The new administrative guidelines went into effect and were subsequently embodied in food stamp legislation passed by Congress.

A second form of legislative response is *goal refinement*. This occurs when steps are taken to make an existing regulation conform more precisely to current congressional sentiment. Following the 1970 reform amendments, administrators issued a regulation in 1971 that required states to take action to encourage eligible nonparticipants to join the food stamp program. When the Minnesota Legal Aid Society and FRAC won a suit against USDA because states were failing to ensure participation of all eligible individuals, as specified in the law, the offending regulation had to be changed.[3] Although Congress had originally directed that participation be ensured, it never really meant it. The law was amended in 1977, and the revised regulations only required states to inform eligible nonparticipants about the program.

Goal assertion takes place when the Congress judges that administrators have exceeded their discretionary grant of authority by putting forward regulations thought to be in defiance of congressional intent. In practical terms, the pertinent regulations often come in the absence of any clear congressional intent. Unlike goal refinement, where Congress acknowledges its grant of discretion, goal assertion occurs when Congress questions both the discretion and the substance of a regulation. This type of reaction took place in 1975, after President Ford ordered his government-wide cutback in budgetary outlays. Included as part of the Ford plan were the proposed food stamp regulations that would have saved the government an estimated $650 million to $1 billion a year by raising the purchase price of the stamps. Congress rejected the administration's contention that it had the authority to reform the program through regulation. In an unusual move, Congress passed a law voiding the regulations.[4]

A fourth kind of congressional reaction is *goal conflict*. This type of reaction occurs when there is congressional activity aimed at either goal refinement or goal assertion. The protagonists, however, fail (at least in the short run) to achieve a change in the law that would modify the existing regulations. Goal conflict differs from goal affirmation in that a significant attempt is made at some point to restructure certain regulations through statute. The majority consensus or apathy of goal affirmation does not exist; rather, one concerned faction prevails over another. In the history of the food stamp program, one of the longest-running cases of goal conflict centered on the issue of striker participation. Ever since administrators, in the absence of clear legislative intent, permitted striking workers to receive stamps, congressional conservatives have proposed amendments outlawing food stamps for workers on strike. This goal was finally accomplished in 1981 with the Reagan administration budget cuts that forced a series of eligibility changes. Newly emerging issues of conflict between congressmen and administrators concern definitions for income and deductions. Liberals fear that the conservative administration will use its regulatory latitude to make the new standards punitive, thereby decreasing the cost of the program.

The differences among these types of reactions are, in large part, a measure of congressional sentiment to extend control over program policy making. Goal affirmation is the most passive congressional role, and it furthers the greatest amount of administrative discretion. At the other extreme is goal assertion, when Congress moves to correct "mistaken" interpretations of administrative discretion. Goal conflict represents something of a middle ground, with sharp disagreement over the agency's discretionary latitude and substantive policy decisions. Goal refining does not reflect a primary concern with excessive administrative discretion. It is better described as an incremental process by which Congress gradually develops its own guidelines to give further specification to administrative policy.

STRATEGIES OF LEGISLATIVE CONTROL

This analysis of legislative response through statute has illuminated only part of the congressional activity aimed at controlling the content of regulations.[5] Congressmen do not always have the option of changing regulations by amending a statute. Yet, even if that option is available, there is an underlying question of strategy. Given the choice, a congressman must ask himself if he will have a better chance of achieving his objectives by specifying policy in the amended legislation or by eschewing a statutory strategy and, instead, waiting to intervene during the rulemaking process.

Legislative Specification. It may seem logical that a congressman seeking certain policy goals will attempt to secure the most specific language possible in a bill and its accompanying legislative report. Yet a congressman pursuing his policy goals must calculate whether or not he is likely to gain enough support for the language he most favors. The congressman's decision as to the amount of specification in the bill is thus based on his opinion of what can win his colleagues' approval. To try to obtain specific statutory language in committee or on the floor and to lose can create a history of intent that will influence administrators *not* to do what the individual congressman would like. If the issue at hand is structured in such a way so that there are fundamentally opposed alternatives, then a congressman may have little choice but to vote for his preferred policy and hope that his side prevails. If the choices evolve around a compromise or series of compromises, where shades of meaning take on added importance, strategic considerations then become central.

When the probability of losing on preferred language appears to be high, a practical strategy may be to seek deliberate ambiguity in phrasing. An example of congressmen trying not to make legislative intent as clear as possible appears in the work registration requirement written into the 1970 food stamp bill. There was enough sentiment in the Agriculture Committees to include a provision in their bills to force food stamp recipients to search for employment. A critical issue in any type of work registration requirement for welfare recipients is the degree to which individuals should be coerced into jobs that are available but not desired. Conservative committee members felt that the language adopted by the House and modified by the conference committee was probably straightforward enough to indicate committee intent for a vigorous work requirement.[6] Worried liberals tried to keep the requirement from being any more specific. Neither conservatives nor liberals pressed for the language they really wanted because victory was somewhat uncertain. "We didn't want to define it too closely and the opposition didn't want to define it too closely," said one committee conservative. Each side accepted the language as the best possible at that time.

Both sides were also aware that administrators could interpret committee intent in various ways. Conservatives, led by Chairman Poage, let FNS know that they did not expect the regulations to put loopholes into the work registration requirement. Liberals, led by Ron Pollack, Kenneth Schlossberg, and Gerald Cassidy, counterattacked by meeting with Jim Springfield, head of the Food Stamp Division in FNS, to tell him what they thought the regulations ought to look like. In the end, Springfield and other administrators decided to issue work registration regulations more in line with the liberals' preferences. The food stamp regulations simply stated that able-bodied participants must accept "suitable" offers of employment. Ostensibly, this requirement would facilitate administrative efficiency, but FNS officials were also unsympathetic to a strict conservative interpretation of the work registration requirement.

Chairman Poage and other conservatives were outraged at FNS's interpretation of congressional intent. After 1971, conservatives repeatedly attempted to put more restrictive language into the law so as to reduce administrators' discretion over the work registration requirement. In 1977 they finally obtained a provision mandating a small number of pilot projects to test a very stringent work requirement.[7] Further provisions for workfare became part of the 1981 law, but the ideological split in the Congress remains over how stiff a requirement is justified. Nevertheless, despite the strong feelings on the question, the initial division on the matter led to a great deal of administrative discretion.

The degree of specification is thus clearly related to the numerical strength of legislators on a committee or in an entire body who share similar views on a given issue. Two other factors that contribute to the level of specificity should also be mentioned. One variable is the age of a program. As a program grows and develops, expected and unforeseen problems arise, more regulations follow, and Congress eventually responds with more detailed legislation directed at solving some of those problems. A second reason for greater legislative specificity in food stamp legislation is the changing nature of Congress. As we shall examine more closely below, both the House and the Senate have moved to reform themselves, and part of this reform spirit has led to a new emphasis on legislative oversight and evaluation. A reflection of this change is the $200,000 staff study of the food stamp program published by the House Agriculture Committee in 1976. A specially recruited staff of ten produced a 560-page study of nine issues confronting the program.[8] The difference this special staff made in the length and detail of the committee's food stamp legislative reports is illustrated by Table 4. The growth of legislative reports into such mammoth documents is important because these volumes amplify congressional intent. Committee members can use the reports to explain what each line in the accompanying bill means, knowing full well that administrators will read such reports closely before issuing regulations. Not all of the material has to do with legislative intent, but recent reports contain extraordinarily detailed analyses of every provision in proposed food stamp legislation.

An example of just how detailed the reports can get is shown in a provision of the 1977 law dealing with Indian reservations. The law

Table 4. Length of Legislative Reports, House
Agriculture Committee

Bill and House report	Length of report
1964, H.R. 10222, Report 1228	54 pages
1967, H.R. 1318, Report 189[a]	32
1970, H.R. 18582, Report 91-1402	37
1976, H.R. 13613, Report 94-1460[a]	868
1977, H.R. 7940, Report 95-464	862
1980, S. 1309, Report 96-788	439
1981, H.R. 3603, Report 97-106[b]	90

[a]This bill did not become law.
[b]The budget resolution set the contours of the policy changes.

permits a tribal organization to run the food stamp program on its own reservation if the secretary of agriculture determines that the state agency "is failing . . . properly to administer such program on such reservation." This portion of the law, surprisingly detailed, lists some of the conditions that must be present in order for a tribe to be able to administer its own food stamp program. However, the legislative report goes even further in specifying those necessary conditions. The report also makes it absolutely clear that it is the intent of Congress that Indian tribes should not run their own programs except as a last resort. The report specifies that a state agency has to refuse to run the reservation program in order for it to be considered "improperly" administered. To make the point more emphatic, the report notes that the committee almost went as far as to forbid completely a tribe from running its own program. In sum, the report and the statute leave almost no discretion for administrators on this small issue of food stamps and Indian reservations.[9]

Greater specification through legislative reports represents to some extent a belief by congressmen that administrators are not sympathetic to those congressmen's goals. Part of the reason the 1976 House Agriculture Committee report was so lengthy was because Chairman Thomas Foley (D.–Wash.) and his liberal aides did not trust Republican administrators to interpret the law fairly according to its intent. The report covered the bill "line-by-line, so that it would control every piece of regulation ever issued," commented one Democratic staffer. Committee reports, like so many committee resources, are more the province of the majority than of the minority. Although minority members can state their views separately, the majority has greater responsibility for determining how detailed the legislative analysis will be.

The strategy of statutory specification is a problematic one. Ideally, a congressman would prefer to control regulations by inserting unequivocal language both in the committee report and in the law itself. But unless one is in the clear majority on a given issue, pushing for specification entails substantial risks. For this type of legislative struggle, it is not a case of better to have tried and failed than to have not tried at all. Instead, the risks must be weighed against those of the alternative strategy.

Intervention. Congressional intervention into rulemaking occurs not only after a bill has just been enacted but also at times when Congress is between reauthorizations. Intervention has both a public and a private side. Public intervention takes place when a member of Congress uses the media, hearings, or other open forums to state his or her case. Private intervention takes place behind the scenes, with legislators personally communicating their wishes to program administrators.

Public intervention by congressmen has been quite common on food stamp issues. Stories fed to or created for the press have been used frequently as leverage against administrators reluctant to conform with the preferences of various congressmen. As noted throughout, much of the public intervention in the program came from the Senate Select Committee on Nutrition and Human Needs. Though abolished in a Senate reorganization in 1977, during its life the committee exercised continuing oversight for food stamp supporters.[10]

The Nutrition Committee was at its peak of influence when it successfully intervened in the rulemaking that followed from the 1970 bill. Among other things, the proposed food stamp regulations raised the purchase price slightly for some recipients and cut off a small percentage of participants from a few states with generous welfare eligibility lines. The hearings orchestrated by McGovern, Schlossberg, and Cassidy effectively put USDA on the defensive. Although administrators had an opportunity to defend themselves, the atmosphere surrounding the hearings and the accompanying press stories made them appear to be a bunch of niggardly bureaucrats willing to take the food out of the mouths of suffering individuals.[11] The Nutrition Committee took a group of regulations, most of them not nearly as malicious as they were made out to be, and gave them the appearance of pettiness and cruelty. The administrators conceded on almost every disputed point in the final regulations.[12]

The private side of legislative intervention into rulemaking encompasses a wide range of activities. It can amount to little more than phone calls to administrators. Messages can also be sent indirectly through staff, lobbyists, or legislative liaison personnel. Congressional communication aimed at influencing regulations is not necessarily hostile or threatening. Committee chairmen and agency administrators have many reasons for wanting to get along with each other. Committee chairmen can affect budgets, reduce administrative discretion, and embarrass or ridicule the agency through public intervention. For their part, administrators can refuse to interpret ambiguous policies in the manner desired by the chairman, be unreceptive to pet projects of committee members, and encourage OMB or the White House to work against particular legislative proposals.[13]

Yet, notwithstanding all the reasons for committees and agencies to want to cooperate with each other, harmony is not always easily achieved. As will be discussed in full in Chapter 6, there has been a low degree of consensual policy making between the Congress and USDA. Personal and ideological differences have accentuated the instinctive wariness over encroachments by the "other" branch. As a result, interveners have been regarded as intruders rather than as partners.

In addition to legislative specification and intervention, a third method of congressional control was the legislative veto. Depending upon the type of legislative veto, regulations would commonly take effect if Congress failed to disapprove of them within an allotted time. During the time prior to the Supreme Court's landmark decision invalidating the legislative veto, Congress did not utilize such a device for controlling the food stamp program.

The Decision Calculus. How do congressmen decide whether or not to pursue legislative specification or intervention? The development of the food stamp program suggests a decision-making framework that is surely common to most domestic policy programs. Congressmen begin, of course, by assessing the varying levels of support for their goals by colleagues, administrators, and the public. They must also consider the patterns of policy making they observe at the committee and agency levels. Is the committee well integrated, generally working toward compromise during markup? Do partisan or ideological reasons make it difficult to work with members on the other side of the aisle or with the individuals running the program at the administrative level? Is the committee-agency relationship consensual in nature, or is it more distant or even hostile?

Beyond the judgment of how others are likely to behave, there is also a question of personal style and ideological commitment. At what point must principle stand above compromise? There are some congressmen, like former Ways and Means Chairman Wilbur Mills, who seem to be born conciliators. But the same would not be said for Jesse Helms, who could never be described as one who "goes along to get along."

With all these factors in mind, a congressman wishing to control the content of regulations must ask if he is likely to win specification of his policies in pending legislation. If the answer is no, or if there is a high degree of uncertainty, he must then ask if he is likely to achieve the same goal through intervention. If this answer is also no, then he must adopt a more defensive strategy. The primary concern becomes to prevent opposing policies from being adopted. If agency discretion is to be feared, then a congressman should want to pursue detailed compromise at the committee level. Policies that give each side some of what it wants, leaving minimal discretion to the agency, is the best solution under such circumstances. If, on the other hand, the committee is the greater obstacle, the best strategy is one of deliberate ambiguity. Ideally, those policies that must be considered should be worded as generally as possible.

The strategies actually adopted by congressmen interested in controlling regulations are important, if little understood, aspects of the legislative process. Congressmen deciding whether to press for detailed statutory language or to hold their fire until they can intervene during rulemaking are engaging in risk assessment. In this light, it is useful to reconsider the stereotypical image of a Congress that habitually passes sloppy, vaguely worded legislation. It is a commonly held belief that legislators deliberately do this so that difficult policy decisions will be placed in the laps of administrators. Morris Fiorina makes the standard case against Congress: "Why [should Congress] take political chances by setting detailed regulations sure to antagonize some political actor or another? Why not require an agency to do the dirty work and then step in to redress the grievances that result from its activities?"[14]

The evidence here suggests that the decision on what to write into statute and what to defer to the regulatory stage is more complicated for congressmen than that. Congressmen do not pass the buck to administrators as a matter of course. Indeed, they sometimes write extraordinarily detailed statutory provisions and legislative reports. The ambiguous wording of certain legislation may have little to do with the desire of congressmen to avoid political heat from those who disagree with them. Rather, the final form of the legislation may represent a calculated decision to pursue policy objectives with more sympathetic administrators or to buy time until the political climate turns more favorable.

INCENTIVES FOR OVERSIGHT

If congressmen are to influence policy making effectively at the administrative level, they must be willing to monitor agency activity conscientiously. This is a crucial assumption, since the conventional wisdom on legislative oversight maintains that congressmen give it relatively low priority. Yet the history of the food stamp program is one of substantial congressional intervention into administrative rulemaking. How does this finding fit with what is known about legislative oversight of the bureaucracy?

There is no common agreement as to what specific legislative activities constitute oversight. Morris Ogul's definition of oversight as "behavior by legislators and their staffs, individually or collectively, which results in an impact, intended or not, on bureaucratic behavior,"[15] recognizes that congressmen exert influence on administrators through many methods not normally labeled as oversight. Clearly, intervention into rulemaking seems to be a basic form of oversight.

Both scholars and congressmen themselves agree that Congress's oversight performance is inadequate. Political scientist John Bibby has called oversight "Congress' neglected function."[16] Would-be reformers have traditionally listed oversight as one of the areas in which Congress must improve itself. And in periodic legislative reform drives, Congress has taken steps to enhance its oversight procedures.[17]

The standard explanation of why Congress devotes so little time and resources to oversight is that the incentive structure is not conducive to it. David Mayhew argues that congressmen's pre-eminent goal is re-election; therefore, it is usually irrational of them to spend time on oversight:

> The important point here is that on measures lacking particu-
> larized benefits the congressmen's intrinsic interest in the
> impact of legislation vanishes. Hence, it is a misallocation of
> resources to devote time and energy to prescription or
> scrutiny of impact unless, again, credit is available for
> legislative maneuvering.[18]

In Mayhew's eyes, congressmen will intervene in the bureaucracy only when they will be able to claim that their actions resulted in direct benefits to their constituents. Not surprisingly, Mayhew regards oversight of program implementation as an activity that usually affords little payoff for the credit-seeking legislator. Instead, congressmen will calculate that their time and that of their staffs can be better spent on passing new laws, on case work, or on campaigning.

In testimony before a congressional committee examining legislative oversight, Nelson Polsby made the same point in even simpler terms: ". . . why doesn't oversight take place [?] I think it is probably because the relevant committee and subcommittee chairmen don't want to, and the reason they don't want to is because they have made some political judgments of their own about what their priorities ought to be."[19] Professor Bibby gave the panel a similar message: "The regularization of oversight will not take place until the Members think it is worth their while to invest time, staff, and other resources in it."[20]

When congressmen do perform oversight and claim credit for it, the reasons traditionally cited are constituency pressure, a desire to embarrass an opposing administration, an ostensible usurpation of power from the executive branch, or a policy problem or scandal that focuses national attention on an agency.[21] Oversight is thus undertaken in response to external provocation or as a means toward narrow partisan gain. It is rarely discussed in terms of a congressman's desires to pursue personal, ideological goals. If good public policy comes about because of oversight, it is a secondary consequence of actions taken primarily for other reasons.

In short, the general conclusion reached by congressional scholars is that legislators are negligent in carrying out their oversight responsibilities. Moreover, this pattern is fully understandable, since the rewards for oversight are usually insignificant. Active attempts at oversight usually have short-term, practical motives. And no theoretical work argues that it is rational behavior for congressmen to expend substantial resources pursuing oversight on a regular basis.

116

Nevertheless, the record of the food stamp program fits poorly with the conventional wisdom. On the one hand, the Agriculture Committees' unwillingness to undertake oversight until alleged food stamp fraud and waste became a national issue in 1974 seems to prove that oversight is infrequent. In fact, the members of the Agriculture Committees and their aides are the first to admit that food stamp oversight has been ignored through the years. "Oversight? There was none," said one veteran staffer on the House side. A long-time Democratic member of the House Agriculture Committee cited the lack of incentives: "The members of this committee aren't that interested. It makes no difference to the farmer if you give them [poor people] stamps or give them cash."

But if the Agriculture Committees' lack of oversight appears to prove the conventional wisdom, the vigorous and continuing legislative intervention by the Senate Nutrition Committee seems to disprove it. If their oversight had been brief or intermittent, it could be considered a short-term response to public opinion or a side effect of partisan conflict. As a select (investigative) committee, the Nutrition Committee was not empowered to write legislation. What influence it could hope for had to come from oversight, and it followed that strategy ceaselessly.[22] It is as if one part of the Congress, the Agriculture Committees, became dysfunctional and another organ was generated to perform its job. Oversight on food stamps was eventually pursued to an exceptional degree once the Agriculture Committees no longer had to be depended upon.

It is possible that this pattern of oversight is anomalous because of the unique features of the food stamp program. How many newly created programs are put under the jurisdiction of congressional committees so uninterested in them?[23] How many programs come under the purview of a committee set up to do little else but oversee them? It is also possible, as will be argued here, that the oversight of the food stamp program has been neither anomalous nor paradoxical. Two lines of thinking guide this thesis. The first is that the Congress is changing and that the increased emphasis on food stamp oversight in later years reflects these changes. Second, the conventional wisdom may not be entirely accurate. It may underestimate the amount of oversight that is done, and it certainly underestimates the incentives for oversight.

The Evolving Congress. Spurred on by public dissatisfaction with Congress, an undeclared war in Vietnam, a seemingly uncontrollable budget, large numbers of new members, and executive branch encroachments on their constitutional duties, both the House and the Senate imposed institutional reforms on themselves in the first half of the 1970s. To meet new needs, the resources that Congress allows itself increased dramatically. The Congressional Budget Office, composed of a substantial staff of economists and other social scientists, was created to go along with a revised budgetary process. Congress formed an Office of Technology Assessment and developed greater overall computer facilities. The staffs of committees, representatives, senators, and the Congressional Research Service grew significantly. Many reforms aimed as well to "democratize" the Congress, and especially the House. In the House, a decentralization of power occurred, with subcommittees taking on added responsibility. Some autocratic and ineffectual House committee chairmen were removed by vote in early 1975, strengthening the influence of less senior representatives.[24] Plans to reorganize committees and their jurisdictions, however, fell far short of initial expectations in both houses.[25]

Congressional reform also touched directly upon the oversight function. The Legislative Reorganization Act of 1970 required that each committee produce a biennial legislative oversight report. More oversight responsibility for the Government Accounting Office was spelled out in this act, as well as in the Congressional Budget and Impoundment Control Act of 1974. In addition, the latter reform encouraged stronger congressional efforts at program evaluation. Finally, a 1974 House committee reform plan authorized each committee to establish oversight subcommittees or require its existing subcommittees to perform oversight in its policy spheres. The resolution provided for some additional funding for committee oversight hearings, specified that oversight findings be separately identified in committee publications, and expanded the oversight jurisdiction of seven committees, enabling them to look into broad policy problems.[26]

Probably more important than any structural change has been a change in attitude within the Congress. Congress is more skeptical of leadership offered by the executive branch. The House and the Senate are more assertive, more willing to fight for what they feel are their rightful duties and powers.[27] Although the first year of the Reagan administration stands in contrast to the pattern of the 1970s, the growing recognition that Congress exercised poor judgment in accepting too much of the Reagan tax program may stimulate increasing legislative independence in the future.

Part of the explanation for greater congressional interest in oversight derives from changes in the regulatory environment. The breadth of government activity through regulation, which was already great, expanded substantially during the 1960s and early 1970s.[28] The sheer quantity of policy decisions made at the regulatory stage forced Congress to pay more attention to what goes on in administrative agencies. Beyond this, however, is an increasingly critical public that has grown weary of big government. Excessive regulation is part of the popular perception of an overextended, inefficient, swollen bureaucracy. This changing public attitude is more concerned with how government performs its tasks and is less committed to the creation of new social programs. There is seemingly more credit to be gained with contemporary voters for investigating (overseeing) what government is doing with the taxpayers' money.

Some evidence suggests that the amount of oversight has increased significantly. Using a narrow operational definition of oversight (congressional hearings, as summarized in the *Daily Digest*), Joel Aberbach has documented a large increase in the oversight activity of both House and Senate committees. Between the Ninety-first Congress (1969–1970) and the Ninety-fourth (1975–1976), House oversight hearings per Congress expanded from 122 days to 267 days. For the Senate, the comparable figures are 81 days in the Ninety-first Congress and 171 days in the Ninety-fourth.[29]

It is more difficult to measure Ogul's broader notion of oversight as any legislative behavior that has an impact on an agency. Many of the types of intervention into rulemaking discussed here cannot be quantified. Nor is it clear that the quality of oversight has improved, although the past decade has seen a greater reliance on professional social scientists and modern evaluative techniques. Reports published by congressional research units and by committees do show more emphasis on measurement and sophisticated analysis of program performance. Still, since political scientists who write about oversight dwell on the lack of it, there are few guidelines to use in evaluating the oversight that does take place.[30]

The growing legislative oversight for food stamps is partly a product of program aging. The program became much more important in the late 1960s as it grew and served more people. Nevertheless, oversight has generally been thought to be episodic rather than significantly correlated with the age of a program. The problems in the food stamp program existed long before extensive oversight was initiated. Although the aging of the program allowed more time for these problems to be "discovered," the oversight was also a product of changes going on within the country and within the Congress.

Why Oversight Is Done. Changes in and about the Congress have stimulated more oversight, but very real incentives for oversight existed prior to this most recent era of reform. The literature on oversight has not given proper emphasis to the reasons why congressmen choose to become involved in oversight, perhaps because the traditional perspective stresses formal committee review of administrative performance.[31] General findings of insufficient congressional oversight may also receive exaggerated support from unrealistic expectations of what can be accomplished through oversight. The mandate contained in the Legislative Reorganization Act of 1946 for Congress to exert "continuous watchfulness" over administrative agencies is commonly cited as if it were a practical standard against which Congress should be judged.[32] Congress can and should do more oversight. But if the broader notion of oversight as legislative intervention is accepted, then more oversight is taking place than is commonly assumed. Consequently, it is important to look beyond the standard explanations of why congressmen engage in oversight. In addition to credit claiming, external pressure, scandal, challenge from the executive branch, and partisan gain,[33] three inducements to oversight are relevant to intervention into the rulemaking process.

First, congressmen take part in activities aimed at influencing administrators because they want to become what may be termed a "policy influential." A policy influential is a senator or representative who is recognized as having substantial power over the formulation of policy for a given issue area. It is natural for a legislator to want to become the leading actor on a particular set of issues. In most cases these issues will coincide with a congressman's committee assignments. The most obvious reward from being a policy influential is its electoral benefit. Extra publicity accrues to the policy influential, making him appear that much more valuable to his constituents.[34] But more than a desire for credit motivates congressmen toward accumulating influence. In taking issue with Mayhew, Lawrence Dodd notes:

> Yet members of Congress generally are not solely preoccupied with reelection. Most members have relatively secure electoral margins. . . . The existence of secure electoral margins thus allows members to devote considerable effort

toward capturing a "power position" within Congress and generating a mystique of special authority that is necessary to legitimize a select decision-making role for them in the eyes of their nominal peers.[35]

Individual congressmen, especially those with some seniority and electoral security, may act more to satisfy the inner drives that push them to seek power and esteem than to achieve re-election. It is easy to identify legislators—for example, Senator Henry Jackson (defense policy) and Senator Russell Long (tax policy)—who have worked assiduously to become dominant influences over their chosen policy areas despite the increasing safeness of their seats. But if a congressman is to protect or increase his standing as a policy influential, he must be highly concerned with administrative regulations. One who exercises influence over legislation is important; one who influences legislation *and* regulations is doubly so. Senator McGovern became a significant figure in the making of food stamp policy more for his intervention into rulemaking than for his role in writing legislation on the Senate Agriculture Committee. If an agency suspects that particular kinds of regulations will cause a congressman to intervene, it is more likely to keep his view in mind when formulating regulations. Over time, successful intervention and the deference of administrators will result in a reputation for influence in agency rulemaking.

Since congressmen seek to amass influence within their respective bodies, it *is* rational for them to expend resources to intervene in the bureaucracy and to conduct other forms of oversight. Contrary to Mayhew's assessment, the lack of particularized benefits does not signal a misallocation of time and energy.[36] Intervention is a direct means to valuable ends (influence and esteem), which in turn enhance re-election chances. Contributions from political action committees flow to those perceived as powerful, and the reputation of being an important force in the Congress hardly hurts back home. Being powerful has its own inner rewards, and the pursuit of power does not have to interfere with activities toward other goals.

A second reason for oversight is ideology. Each legislator has certain policy preferences about which he feels quite strongly. To see that those preferences become actual policy, he makes use of the legislative tactics at his disposal, including intervention into rulemaking. This is hardly a startling finding; yet, surprisingly, ideology receives little emphasis in most studies of legislative behavior. Although roll call analysts have focused upon ideology,[37] other students of the Congress have tended to ignore or downplay its explanatory value.

One scholar who has treated the ideological motive as central to congressional behavior is Richard Fenno. In *Congressmen in Committees*, Fenno observes that members of the House have three primary goals: re-election, influence within the House, and "good" public policy.[38] Which is most important? Fenno writes, "each congressman has his own mix of priorities and intensities—a mix which may, of course, change over time."[39] The nature of a congressman's committee assignments is crucial to that mix: "House members . . . match their individual patterns of aspiration to the diverse patterns of opportunity presented by House committees."[40]

Both Fenno and Mayhew underestimate the degree to which the pursuit of "good" public policy can complement the pursuit of re-election. For reasons of conceptual clarity, it is obviously useful to distinguish between such goals. Yet in the real world they easily blend together. There is some credit to be had in almost all policy areas. On practically any given matter, a congressman can pursue intervention, for whatever reasons, with the assurance that some audience will be grateful.

In the case of food stamps, there have been a large number of congressmen who cared little about the program, a large number who cared some, and a small band who cared greatly. As is probably typical of most issues in the Congress, it is this small band that has conducted the bulk of the oversight. The actions of people like Leonor Sullivan, Robert Kennedy, Robert Michel, George McGovern, and Jesse Helms cannot be explained away as calculated efforts to win support among constituents, to appease interest groups, or to amass influence within the Congress. These may have been considerations, but in each case, involvement with food stamps was consistent with a larger range of interests. For none of them did food stamps simply represent an obligation to a state or district constituency. Their activity often transcended their normal committee responsibilities. They sought out the issue and worked on it with great energy, imagination, and fervor. Although their individual views differed, these members of Congress were moved to act because they believed current food stamp policy to be incompatible with their own prescription for a fair and just society. Each had a vision of what "good" food stamp policy should be, and each intervened to try to make that vision a reality. Ideology catalyzed their oversight.

Third, and finally, congressional staffs are an inducement for oversight. Again, the most common explanation given for the lack of oversight is that congressmen can expend their time more profitably on other activities. Since oversight is not always the most visible activity, and since congressmen have many other pressing concerns, it is easy to ignore that responsibility. Assigning a skilled staff to do the supporting work for oversight is a way for congressmen to have their cake and eat it too. And it became all the easier to do this as Congress rapidly expanded its staff resources throughout its organizational structure.

Staff members are often "entrepreneurs," individuals looking out for issues that their boss can make a "profit" on.[41] Staffers from the congressman's office, committees, or other units can do the ground work, learning what is going on in the bureaucracy and out in the field. Their findings can be publicly "discovered" by the congressman, who can then take credit for protecting the public interest. But even though they may act as entrepreneurs, staffers are hardly independent actors. In his careful study of congressional staffs, Michael Malbin found that aides are faithful in representing their bosses' views.[42] When staffs do conduct oversight of administrative agencies, their actions are aimed at influencing policy in accord with their congressmen's interests. Malbin also concluded that growth of personal staffs was directly responsible for increased congressional oversight: "Congress is not so passive today, thanks largely to its staff."[43]

This history of the food stamp program supports Malbin's thesis. Entrepreneurial staffers like David Swoap and John Kramer moved vigorously on their own, but clearly in accordance with the policy views of their bosses. The repeated references in this work to intervention by the Senate Nutrition Committee has really been a shorthand way of describing the intervention by William Smith, Kenneth Schlossberg, Gerald Cassidy, and Marshall Matz, the principal food stamp aides. These four staffers could not have acted more energetically and could not have been more committed to the success of the food stamp program. Even if the committee members did not have "better" things to spend their time on, these men were the real interveners and overseers.

For these reasons, as well as for those usually given, oversight is performed more consistently than is thought. As Ogul points out, much of the oversight that takes place is done *latently*. That is, "since the legislators' primary focus is typically elsewhere than on oversight, the general obligation to oversee will tend to be fulfilled mainly as other purposes are being served."[44] In the case of the food stamp program, the oversight that began to expand significantly between 1967 and 1969 can only be understood against the larger backdrop of food stamp politics. Oversight of the program cannot be divorced from the desires of individual congressmen to pursue influence, re-election, and ideological objectives.

The rulemaking process stimulates oversight. If a congressman is to achieve his primary goals, then he must be ready to intervene in the rulemaking process. The regulatory stage can be regarded as something of an appeals court, presenting congressmen with a second opportunity to accomplish what cannot be gained during committee markup. Policy making is continuous and incremental, and legislators pursuing their own mix of goals will often find it worth their while to intervene in administrative rulemaking.

CONCLUSION

The extensive legislative intervention into food stamp rulemaking during the last fifteen years or so has significant implications for the critical views of Kenneth Culp Davis,[45] Theodore Lowi,[46] and others on congressional policy making. During the period beginning with the pilot projects and extending into 1967, congressional behavior on food stamps did fit Davis's observation that Congress delegates authority by telling agencies, "Here is the problem. Deal with it."[47] But congressional involvement in food stamp policy making began to change around 1967. By 1969 an entirely different congressional role had taken shape. Since that time, Congress's attitudes has been more, "Here's the problem. We're watching to see what you do."

The shift toward legislative involvement in rulemaking means that Congress has ceased to be a silent partner in the operation of the food stamp program. Congress has not eliminated substantial grants of discretion, although it has certainly curtailed them over time. The highly important decisions made by administrators under their discretionary authority between 1969 and 1971 were the result not of congressional indifference but of congressional disagreement over program goals. This indecision opened the way for congressmen to intervene in the hope of moving administrators to do what the full Congress would not. No longer could Congress be described as unconcerned with the administration of the food stamp program.

Lack of congressional agreement over program goals, and the consequent lack of specificity in statutory language, are surely chronic conditions of the American political system. Intervention into rulemaking, aside from being a primary means by which congressional intent is amplified, represents to some degree a continuation of the disagreements and conflicts of the legislative process into the administrative realm. Subsequent legislation allows Congress the opportunity to refine, resolve, and agree upon program goals that have come into question through the issuance of regulations.

Although Congress has become more assertive, the basic question of how legislative intent can be best expressed remains unresolved. Congress, if it desired, could make its intent more explicit and widely understood throughout the life of a program. Obviously, the legislative record cannot anticipate all problems. Nevertheless, congressional committees have the resources to create a more thorough legislative record than is often the case. When the House Agriculture Committee wanted to institute greater control over the food stamp program, it devoted the money and staff to produce studies of 860 pages, as opposed to the 30-page reports of earlier years.

Beyond the capabilities that already exist, procedures could be institutionalized to solve some of the problems of unclear intent. Program officials, support staff from the Library of Congress, Budget Office, and General Accounting Office, and outside consultants could play a much greater role in markup sessions and the subsequent writing of reports than they do now. Their analysis of the deficiencies in the drafts of statutes and reports could be used to force decisions where intent is ambiguous.

It seems evident, however, that committees choose a desired, rather than a maximum, level of clarity and degree of comprehensiveness in their intent. They do not generally go to the limits of their knowledge and expertise. As has been emphasized, members of committees cannot always agree on their intent; at the same time, they recognize that there will be opportunities later to intervene and rewrite legislation. For the legislator pursuing influence or ideological goals, strategic choices must be made as to how his objectives can best be achieved. He may find it preferable to define intent later rather than sooner.

The findings here also have important implications for the study of congressional oversight and legislative behavior. Congress is much more involved in overseeing the bureaucracy than is commonly assumed. In part, congressional scholars find little oversight because they define it away. Too often it is viewed as a specific and formal activity, largely dependent on committee hearings. As Ogul asserts, though, it is a much broader enterprise, often indistinct from other legislative pursuits. The repeated intervention into food stamp rulemaking reflects a serious commitment by individual legislators to see to it that their views of congressional policy are carried out.

Despite the extensive research on Congress, the models of legislative man that can be drawn from the literature still seem inadequate. Although scholars such as Mayhew, Dodd, and Fenno have skillfully analyzed the distinct motives that underlie congressional behavior, none of their works fully explains the patterns that emerge from the history of the food stamp program. Congressmen regard their goals not as discrete pursuits but rather as intertwined and frequently complementary objectives. Rational congressional man seeks to allocate his resources so that he can pursue re-election at the same time he seeks influence and good public policy.

6

THE ADMINISTRATOR'S ENVIRONMENT AND ADMINISTRATIVE DISCRETION

POLITICAL SCIENTISTS USUALLY explain policy outcomes as the products of some type of policy subsystem. For a welfare program like food stamps, the dominant actors would seemingly be congressional committee members and agency administrators. Assumptions about the role of interest groups are more problematic, since the literature on policy subsystems has been built almost entirely on cases involving traditional farm, labor, and business groups. Yet, the history of the food stamp program shows that administrators must also contend with client groups when they go through the rulemaking process.

CLIENT GROUPS AND SOCIAL SERVICES REGULATIONS

The creation of the food stamp program in 1961 owes little to interest group activity. By the late 1960s, however, pro–food stamp groups had established an extensive lobbying network, and in 1977 former food stamp activists were running the program for the Carter administration. This transformation in such a relatively short time is far from an isolated phenomenon, for it mirrors a larger pattern of public interest group politics. During the late 1960s and early 1970s, many new public interest lobbies emerged to work on a variety of issues.[1]

Interest groups working for the civil rights and antiwar movements proved to others that citizen advocacy can have a political impact.[2] Indeed, the first food stamp lobbyists had formerly been active in the civil rights movement. By the end of the 1960s, though, the type of strategy exemplified by the Poor People's March on Washington gave way to other forms of food stamp advocacy. The public interest groups that started around this time put less emphasis on demonstrations and concentrated more on litigation and traditional means of legislative and administrative lobbying.[3] Wishing to appeal to a broad audience, including the philanthropic foundations that provided much of their early seed money, most public interest groups showed a commitment to working within the system.

Although the new public interest lobbies behaved along more conventional lines than the protest-oriented groups, they still differed in some important respects from established Washington lobbies. The hunger lobby, for example, has never placed a premium on maintaining friendly relations with those responsible for the program. CNI, FRAC, and other food stamp groups have fought openly with USDA officials, skillfully using the media to portray themselves as the good guys and program administrators as the villains.[4] Their continuing outrage and unremitting criticism made it difficult for early USDA administrators to deal with them. As one food stamp advocate put it, "What's the responsibility of a public interest group? We're not there just to act like another congressman and compromise all the issues away." When one department official sought out a hunger lobbyist to ask why USDA never received any credit for the good things it did, he was told bluntly, "We're in the business of criticizing and not in the business of patting people on the back."

The contentiousness between client groups and administrators has surely not been due to the attitudes of food stamp advocates alone. For their part, administrators did little to foster good relations. Various officials, particularly Howard Davis, Orville Freeman, Clifford Hardin, Earl Butz, and Edward Hekman, were suspicious and often resentful of these organizations. Possibly they were not skillful enough, or committed enough, to persuade these groups to work with USDA in a more constructive manner. Clearly, they did not go as far as they could have to work with the food stamp lobbies.

It is commonly expected that agencies and their client groups will not only refrain from open hostility but will actually work together as partners. Political scientists have gone so far as to claim that client groups eventually "capture" regulatory bodies as part of the natural life cycle of Washington politics.[5] But even if public interest groups are not expected to capture social service agencies, there is still plenty of reason for a cooperative relationship to develop. From the viewpoint of any interest group, it is desirable to become an *institutionalized* part of the administrative process. An institutionalized group is considered a legitimate representative of agency clients and is consulted regularly by administrators. Much of the interaction between agency and interest group takes place out of the public eye. This type of informal but close working relationship offers interest groups a means of bringing their views and data directly to the attention of policy makers. From the perspective of agency administrators, client groups can be regarded as potential sources of political support.[6] As Francis Rourke writes, "it is essential to every agency's power position to have the support of attentive groups whose attachment is grounded on an enduring tie."[7] When this type of relationship exists, Hugh Heclo notes, "The influence of both participants is increased."[8]

Despite the advantages of such a partnership, this kind of relationship existed between food stamp groups and USDA only during the Carter years. Several reasons may explain why an interest group and an administrative agency may not develop a relationship in the manner suggested by Rourke, Heclo, and others. A principal reason is that interest groups must try to avoid co-optation. For public interest groups, their openly critical stance toward government is essential to their credibility. If the price of privileged access to an agency is the inability to articulate major policy differences, a group will likely refuse to pay that price and work instead with its allies in Congress.

Interest groups representing poor people have an additional problem in that their constituency is hardly a cohesive bloc to be feared by politicians. Since neither FRAC nor CNI has food stamp recipients as members, they have less in the way of political support to offer agencies than do trade associations or most other private interest groups. And although it makes sense for administrators to want outside support for their agency and policies, it is also natural for them to want to protect their autonomy. Food stamp administrators have jealously guarded their own authority to make decisions over food stamp policy. Finally, social service agencies seem highly responsive to election results. For a program like food stamps, switches between liberal and conservative presidents can be crucial in determining the nature of the relationship between client groups and FNS.

Food stamp groups surely hope that over time norms will develop in such a way as to further a cooperative relationship no matter who is in office. The strategy of influence adopted by these groups lays the groundwork for an ongoing partnership while it maximizes their short-term influence and avoids co-optation.[9] The core of their philosophy, like that of so many other effective Washington lobbies, is the power of information. There are two critical elements to this part of their strategy. First, the Washington staff members must possess high levels of expertise in their policy fields. Aside from political support, information is the only other asset lobbyists reelly have to offer agency administrators. Since administrators are themselves knowledgeable in their fields, lobbyists must have an unusually good grasp of program operations if they are to be taken seriously.

For Bob Greenstein, Ron Pollack, and other food stamp lobbyists, expertise was their entrée into the bureaucracy. They used their sophisticated knowledge of the program to establish lines of communication with officials during the Nixon administration. That expertise was also a source of their influence in working with the Nutrition Committee, the media, and other sympathetic interest groups. Finally, it was Greenstein's superior knowledge of the food stamp program that helped persuade Bob Bergland to choose him to oversee the program for the Carter administration.

The second, related aspect of their information strategy is to get issues out into the open. The ability of FRAC and CNI to bring proposed regulations and imminent regulatory changes to the attention of those interested in food stamp policy is impressive. Even though their memberships do not include food stamps recipients, these organizations do reach a national constituency of activists and grassroots groups who strongly support the program. They translate the confusing language of the *Federal Register* into clear-cut political analysis of the consequences that would result from the regulations under consideration. The frequency of CNI's *Nutrition Week* gives individuals outside of Washington a thorough, reliable regulatory monitoring device. In the past FRAC has published handouts as need be, sending them to individuals on its mailing list. During the year and one-half that President Carter's welfare reform proposal was being debated, FRAC produced sixteen mailings that, among other things, identified the changing proposals concerning the fate of the food stamp program. Just recently FRAC started publishing a monthly newspaper, *Foodlines*, which covers an expanded range of nutrition and welfare issues. In sum, FRAC and CNI are the communications link for those concerned with food stamp issues and the catalysts for grassroots lobbying.[10]

FRAC's and CNI's aggressiveness in providing detailed information to the public as a means of stimulating pressure on Washington is part of a larger change in interest group tactics. For years, the traditional portrait of lobbies as friendly "service bureaus" to sympathetic congressmen seemed to hold true.[11] Of course, lobbies still provide their allies with data and political support, but they are now much more willing to try actively to influence fence sitters and even opponents. Washington newsletters, "action alert" mailings, membership telephone networks, widespread dissemination of voting records, and direct mail solicitations by political action committees and citizen groups are all common means of maximizing pressure on policy makers by publicizing issues.

The influence of the food stamp groups has also been enhanced by their focus on the whole of government rather than on any one of its parts. Like so many other effective Washington lobbies, they are adept at moving back and forth between Congress, the courts, and the executive branch as the circumstances dictate.[12] When they fail at one branch, they go to another as an appeals court. They have also worked with one branch to try to influence other principals. During the Nixon administration they pushed congressmen to intervene into rulemaking. Later, when sympathetic administrators were in charge of the food stamp program for Jimmy Carter, they worked closely with FNS to develop legislative strategy.

Although many of the early food stamp groups were short-lived, FRAC and CNI have survived for over a decade and represent a stable source of advocacy for program recipients. The Reagan administration budget cuts have threatened both groups, since each has received a good deal of federal funding. CNI's Washington staff is still supported primarily by subscriptions to *Nutrition Week*; any loss of training grants should not affect its lobbying efforts. FRAC, more dependent on federal funds, has at least taken some first steps (such as charging for its publications) toward expanding its funding base. Ironically, liberal public interest groups have been helped in one important respect by the Reagan administration: Their memberships and donations increased sharply as soon as Reagan was elected.[13] CNI has tried to tap liberals' fear and dislike of Reagan with a direct mail campaign. Their fund-raising letter, signed by well-known consumer advocate Esther Peterson, pleads, "Please give as soon as you can. Jesse Helms is already sharpening his knife for the next series of budget cuts."

The effectiveness and relative stability of these groups stands in pointed contrast to the insignificance of citizen participation efforts in food stamp policy making. Beginning with the Economic Opportunity

Act of 1964 and its mandate for "maximum feasible participation," the federal government made a concerted attempt to improve client representation before administrative agencies. By the late 1970s there were over 225 public participation programs of various types.[14] The rationale for requiring public hearings, workshops, or whatever was that certain segments of an agency's constituency were chronically unrepresented. Whereas businesses and trade associations had the financial incentives to become involved in agency rulemaking or project planning, ordinary citizens were less likely to organize.

The citizen participation principle was at the same time an acknowledgment that pluralism did not exist in fact and that it was a desirable goal that government ought to promote.[15] If those affected by government policies did not organize on their own, then the government had an affirmative responsibility to encourage their participation. Citizen participation programs have generally fallen short of their lofty goal of democratizing the administrative process. Nothing in the statutory authorizations requires bureaucrats to share their power with citizens, and the programs often turn into exercises in symbolic politics. Walter Rosenbaum, a long-time student of citizen participation, writes that "few programs apparently have worked well. Some are rituals; many are moribund."[16]

The citizen participation program for food stamps, set up on a voluntary basis by FNS during the Carter administration, proved to be little more than a gesture toward real citizen involvement in agency rulemaking. It was an all too typical case of middle-level bureaucrats showing the flag at different spots around the country; the process itself had very little to do with the actual writing of regulations in Washington. Yet, at the same time, the food stamp lobbies in the capital were directly involved in the drafting of regulations. The goals of citizen participation were thus being achieved by traditional Washington-based lobbying, not through the public hearings instituted by FNS.

Citizen participation programs ought not to be abandoned. At least some programs have worked, and others may improve over time if agencies make a more serious commitment to them.[17] Yet the food stamp experience shows that interest groups in Washington have provided considerably more effective representation for the chronically unrepresented than FNS's public hearings. The conclusion that must be reached is that if the federal government truly wants to promote pluralism, then direct grants to poor people's groups like CNI and FRAC ought to be continued.

THE FOOD STAMP ISSUE NETWORK

To describe the complexities of the policy-making process, scholars have often resorted to the "policy subsystem" concept.[18] Each policy area is said to have a recurring set of participants who interact over time in trying to shape program outcomes. For many years the boundaries of a subsystem seemed easily defined. Douglass Cater described the sugar subsystem in the following terms:

> Political power within the sugar subgovernment is largely vested in the Chairman of the House Agriculture Committee who works out the schedule of quotas. It is shared by a veteran civil servant, the director of the Sugar Division in the U.S. Department of Agriculture, who provides the necessary "expert" advice for such a complex marketing arrangement. Further advice is provided by Washington representatives of the domestic beet and cane sugar growers, the sugar refineries, and the foreign producers.[19]

A policy subsystem, or "iron triangle," thus consisted of a handful of key committee members, agency administrators, and lobbyists. The typical subsystem was stable, even though some of the players might move back and forth to different corners of the triangle. Within each of these private little worlds, policy making was carried out in a cooperative, consensual manner.

As noted earlier, Hugh Heclo has criticized the notion of iron triangle subsystems as being outdated and incomplete. Instead, he offers the concept of an "issue network."[20] Although he acknowledges that it is difficult to describe in any detail what an issue network looks like, he emphasizes some critical characteristics. Issue networks are broader and more open than iron triangles. Also, membership is based not merely on position but on technical competence as well. To go beyond Heclo's basic outline, it is necessary to examine individual issue networks carefully. The food stamp case study offers not only an opportunity to color in a more complete picture of a contemporary issue network, but it also affords a chance to assess the impact of issue network politics on policy making.

One aspect of policy subsystems that seems little changed is the ease with which the various actors move from one job to another in the issue network. Important figures in the history of the food stamp pro-

133

gram have frequently moved from one point in the subsystem to another: Jim Springfield went from USDA to the House Agriculture Committee; John Kramer went from public interest advocacy to join the House Agriculture Committee; Kenneth Schlossberg and Gerald Cassidy left the Nutrition Committee to start their own lobbying and consulting firm on food and nutritional issues; Rod Leonard went from program administrator to the Children's Foundation, and then he started CNI; and Robert Greenstein left CNI to go to USDA, subsequently coming back to public interest lobbying. Issue networks are still relatively small worlds where personal familiarity and professional reputations lead to job offers within the subsystem. For a welfare policy area, where there are no lucrative jobs in the private sector, this kind of movement back and forth seems relatively innocuous. In many other policy areas, where well-paying jobs in trade associations and corporations may be available to a person with valuable government experience, the movement of "in-and-outers" remains troublesome.

In other respects, the food stamp issue network shows important differences when compared with the long-held image of iron triangles. The most serious criticism of iron triangles was that they develop into independent fiefdoms. In Cater's words, "subgovernments flourish and grow autonomous. They become arrogant in their jurisdictions, defiant of efforts to form a larger consensus than each finds sufficient to its needs."[21] As Heclo observes, analysts have concluded that these subsystems are even beyond the control of the White House: "A President or presidential appointee may occasionally try to muscle in, but few people doubt the capacity of these subgovernments to thwart outsiders in the long run."[22] Heclo points out that presidents have trouble exerting leadership over issue networks because of the technical complexity of individual programs.[23]

The history of the food stamp program reveals a policy subsystem that is far less autonomous than either Cater or Heclo contends is typical. At times, of course, members of the subsystem have made food stamp policy with minimal outside interference. Overall, though, the food stamp issue network has not been an autonomous force impervious to White House influence or swings in the nation's ideological pendulum. When presidents or their appointees have so chosen, they have had an immediate and direct impact on crucial policy decisions. The differences for food stamp policy making between a Butz and a

Bergland or a Carter and a Reagan have been dramatic. Likewise, changes in public opinion have strongly influenced food stamp policy making.

The food stamp issue network is relatively open rather than tightly knit. It also lacks the unity of purpose associated with iron triangles. A common outlook and cooperative working relationship among the committees, USDA, and the lobbyists has been the exception and not the rule during the life of the program. Sometimes two sides of the triangle have worked against a third. At other times congressional committee members have worked at cross purposes because of their ideological differences. Is the food stamp network a "mutual self-help arrangement"?[24] It hardly appears so. Instead, it is composed of shifting coalitions and principled infighters.

The most commonly shared characteristic of participants in the food stamp area turns out to be expertise. This has always been an important factor, as Cater's description of the sugar subgovernment indicates. As programs grow more and more complex, expertise in the field is more and more a prerequisite for admittance to a network. The food stamp policy area is far less technical than energy or defense for example, but it still requires detailed knowledge. A competent food stamp analyst must understand the interaction between AFDC, housing, and energy benefits and food stamp allotments. He or she must learn how to judge computer projections of participation and cost, since such forecasts are quite sensitive to the performance of the economy. Projections based on changes in eligibility criteria are also problematic. Workfare and work disincentives for higher-income participants are other complicated issues. Technical mastery of the program must thus come with experience or academic study, and the most influential participants in the network have often served long apprenticeships.

Developing an accurate description of issue network politics is important because of the assumption that subsystems largely control public policy. Autonomous issue networks do not seem justified by common interpretations of democratic theory. Yet the food stamp network has not been characterized by total independence. Nor is it a cooperative arrangement fueled by mutual self-interest. The network has always exhibited a healthy division between liberals and conservatives. The expertise of network participants does give them authority over many program decisions. Still, major policy decisions have not been out of the control of the White House, and elections and public opinion have made a difference. In short, the food stamp issue network has not been unresponsive to the political environment that surrounds it.

Welfare issue networks are certainly different in some respects from those in other policy areas. All issue areas have their unique attributes, but the analysis here points up the shortcomings of a general concept that is intended to cover government as a whole. Other issue areas surely have networks that are sharply divided along ideological lines or are highly responsive to changes in the presidency. There is simply not enough research on contemporary issue networks to warrant acceptance of the common generalizations about their autonomy, influence, or unity. Their differences may be more numerous than their similarities.

INTERPRETING CONGRESSIONAL INTENT

If the food stamp issue network were a cooperative, consensus-seeking subsystem, it would be relatively easy for administrators to interpret congressional intent. In their ongoing interaction with key committee members, FNS officials could discuss important regulatory issues with them. Unclear intent or divided opinion could be settled satisfactorily through negotiations before pertinent regulations were actually written.[25]

Since food stamp policy making has not proceeded in this fashion, FNS administrators have had to decide for themselves the amount of consultation they would seek before preparing regulations. For their part, congressmen have not always waited to be asked; they have intervened in the rulemaking process when and where they have seen fit. In the end, though, the administrators must decide how to translate their interpretation of intent into program regulations.

How that interpretation takes place has direct bearing on the familiar debate over administrative responsibility. Are administrators capable on their own (as Carl Friedrich suggested) of developing policies that make maximum use of their technical knowledge while still conforming to popular sentiment?[26] When deference to administrators' expertise is granted, can their self-restraint be relied upon as a sufficient check on irresponsible interpretations of the congressional mandate? Or, alternatively (as Herman Finer suggested), must there be strong external controls over the actions of administrators to prevent abuses of power?[27] Should agency officials view their responsibilities narrowly and search for congressional guidance to the maximum feasible degree?

In practical terms, administrators must come to grips with this issue each time they go through the rulemaking process. It is at the will of the Congress, through the delegation of authority, that agencies have the power to make policy decisions so that congressional goals may be carried out. Congress, however, does not neatly divide up policy questions into those that it will decide by itself and those that administrators will decide. The line between the two is indistinct; administrators must try to judge where they have legitimate discretion and where Congress has expressed its will.[28]

Interpretation problems arise because of "defects" in legislation passed by Congress. These defects lead to administrative interpretations that may or may not please interested congressmen. One of the most troubling types of statutory defects is a failure of goal agreement. In such cases, intent is not clear because the Congress cannot reconcile its members' views of what intent should be.[29] Wording is passed sometimes *because* it is ambiguous. A second and more common defect in legislation results from Congress's inability to anticipate all of the situations that administrators will eventually face. It is one of the very purposes of administrative agencies to have the flexibility to adapt policy to unforeseen problems. Anticipation defects may be due to truly unique and unexpected exigencies. On the other hand, the unanticipated problem may simply point to a lack of comprehensive analysis on the part of congressional committees.

The lack of specification is a third kind of legislative defect. Again, it is a traditional function of administrative agencies to fill in the unwritten details of legislation. Furthermore, the amount of specification may vary from one section to another in the same law. A bill passed by Congress may contain no general principle of what is or is not within the boundaries of acceptable administrative discretion. Lack of specification may stem from a lack of congressional concern or interest for the different issues in a policy area. Committees and subcommittees choose priorities when considering legislation. The structure of hearings, staff assignments, and markup time are all indications of the intensity of concern for the separate questions that a committee must deal with in each bill. This allocation of committee resources over time is inextricably linked to the levels of specification in legislation.

Any one or all three of these overlapping categories of legislative defects present administrators with a similar decision. How much discretion is warranted by each defect? To what extent is it legitimate to set new policy, to depart significantly from past practices? The decision of agency officials as to what their administrative responsibility entails on a particular regulation is not simply a matter of conscience or personal preference. Such decisions take place within the context of internal and external constraints.[30] Organizations develop their own "culture," and individuals come to adapt to bureaucratic norms and routines. As a program grows and becomes more complex, regulatory decisions may have to go through more layers of clearance and thus be affected by more people.[31] Growth in organizational complexity has certainly changed the way food stamp regulations are written. Most significantly, the agriculture secretary's office has gradually become more involved in overseeing food stamp rulemaking.

A bureau's external environment includes its relationships with congressional committees and client groups—relationships that have varied considerably in the life of the food stamp program. On controversial regulatory issues, the White House and public opinion become important constraints on agency decisions. Bureaucrats are very much aware of who outside the agency is likely to be watching their actions and cannot help but be influenced by that knowledge.

An additional factor in explaining regulatory decision making is the individual character of administrators. Their "bureaucratic personalities"—springing from their own ambitions, conflicts, and other psychological drives—affect their propensity to take risks.[32] The ideology of administrators is similarly related to such choices. Their own visions of what a program should be help them to define acceptable regulatory alternatives.

Administrators' judgments of internal and external constraints and their bureaucratic personalities thus act to structure the interpretation of intent. An administrator must begin by defining the boundaries of acceptable administrative discretion.[33] Usually, one or more policy options will be unquestionably "safe" choices. These alternatives will displease the fewest legislators and undoubtedly fall within the intent of Congress. An administrator, though, will not always regard the safe choices as the best policies.

In selecting a policy option that is not safe, an administrator runs certain risks. The wider his interpretation of the discretion available, the greater the chance that Congress will later rescind or alter his actions through some method of legislative control.[34] When Congress believes that an administrator has exceeded his grant of discretion, actions aimed at goal assertion (or resulting in goal conflict) are likely to develop. The risk to the administrator is greater than just having the disputed regulation changed by Congress. Congress may also move to assert more general control over the agency by limiting the administrator's overall discretionary authority.

Under what circumstances are administrators likely to seek the higher-risk regulatory choices that reflect a broad interpretation of the discretion open to them? In the case of food stamps, the broadest interpretations of discretion have come when the greatest public attention has been focused on the program. During the period of decidedly liberal public opinion (1967–1971), administrators made their boldest regulatory reforms. Strong public sentiment offers administrators at least some protection and reduces the risk of congressional reprisals. Yet there is no sure method of assessing the intensity of public opinion or the strength of possible congressional reactions. Congress can reassert itself, reducing discretion and applying pressure toward future administrative regulations without appearing to change the basic thrust of agency policy.

An administrator can reduce risk by requesting congressional action to remedy a legislative defect. This is not always a practical solution, but on major policy issues an amendment to the law might be desirable. Most administrators, however, will not want Congress to interfere any more than necessary in their programs. V. O. Key's assessment, written nearly forty years ago, still holds true today: "Government agencies hesitate to seek modifications from Congress. They will rather indulge in improvisations and patiently endure the oddest kinds of legal limitation. The reason is obvious. They never know what will emerge from the legislative mill once it begins to turn."[35]

A middle ground for an administrator between deciding alone and asking for a legislative solution is informal consultation. Consultation with committee members would also meet Herman Finer's standard for administrative responsibility.[36] Further legislative specification can be sought through consultation to ensure that the "will of the people" is carried out by program administrators. Food stamp administrators have occasionally sought consultation, but on the whole they have tended to shy away from it. In line with Carl Friedrich's thinking, the bold regulatory moves in response to public opinion could instead be cited as evidence of administrative responsibility.[37] Yet administrators have not been uniformly responsive to public opinion; their decisions have been less expansive during conservative times.

In the history of the food stamp program, there has simply not been any well-defined norm as to what constitutes the proper level of administrative responsibility. During different periods of rulemaking administrators have rendered varying judgments as to where the boundaries of discretion fall. Can it be said that they ever abused their power or acted irresponsibly? No, their expansive interpretations of their discretion always had some outside support. Still, they did interpret their mandate liberally at times, substituting their own judgment where intent was unclear or contested. Food stamp administrators have anticipated reactions to their regulations but have not negotiated permission for them.

The question remains as to why administrators have not sought informal consultation on a more frequent basis. To some degree, their reluctance has been a function of the partisanship and ideological differences that have separated the key actors in the two branches. In addition, however, there is the question of autonomy. The more an administrator seeks guidance from Congress, the less independent he is. An official's own importance and authority decrease as deference to Congress increases. Edward Hekman, Clifford Hardin, and Howard Davis all guarded their positions carefully and did only what was unmistakably necessary in terms of legislative consultation. Although there are powerful incentives for bureaucrats to cooperate with legislators, the instinct to protect autonomy is also powerful. In writing regulations, food stamp administrators have been willing to take risks by avoiding consultation and interpreting intent on their own. Various administrators have perceived the boundaries of their discretion differently, but all have guarded their authority within those boundaries.

HOW MUCH DISCRETION?

An empirical analysis of Congress, USDA, and food stamp regulations must inevitably give way to more normative concerns. Within our form of government, what *should* be the pattern of legislative-agency interaction for optimally rational and effective public policy? At the outset of this study, two opposing points of view on the question of delegation of authority were described. One position, exemplified by Theodore Lowi's *The End of Liberalism*, holds that Congress has given up too much authority to administrative agencies.[38] Inordinate grants of discretion wrongly permit critical policy decisions to be made by administrators. The alternative view, represented by works such as Joseph Harris's *Congressional Control of Administration*, prescribes a relationship that allows for substantial discretion while discouraging congressional intervention in administrative policy making.[39] Congress must respect the authority of administrators to make decisions within the boundaries of significant grants of discretion.

What, then, can be learned from the food stamp program concerning the proper limits of discretion? How much discretion is, in fact, desirable?[40] One's answer to this question should preferably be divorced from ideological sentiments toward the program. Such objectivity, unfortunately, is rather difficult to achieve. No matter how impartial one tries to be, a liberal who favors generous welfare benefits (as does the author) will be much more tempted to conclude that the sweeping Hardin administrative reforms of 1969 were issued through acceptable discretionary authority. A conservative might think otherwise, taking note of the congressional disagreement at the time and the lack of established legislative intent.

The philosophical problem of whether or not social scientists can conduct value-free research (and create value-free standards of policy evaluation) cannot be resolved within the framework of this study. At the very least, though, the values underlying evaluation can be made explicit. Two standards are considered here to be of overriding importance in evaluating food stamp policy. First, is the program easily accessible to those who are in need of its services? Second, is the assistance provided great enough to make a meaningful improvement in the lives of those who need it? It is to be hoped that these standards are logical and common-sensical criteria to evaluate any type of welfare program.

By these standards the food stamp program deserves generally high marks. The elimination of the purchase price in 1977 removed the last major impediment to participation. The food stamp program must be considered to be highly accessible to those who fall below its income eligibility line.[41] The level of welfare benefits can also be evaluated favorably. Of course, any administrative decision that determines need has an arbitrary quality to it. There is no doubt, though, that food stamp allotments do make a substantial difference in the standard of living of program participants.[42]

Yet positive evaluation of current policies still does not fully answer the question of how well the system worked in creating those policies. Many needy individuals went without stamps for a long time because of decisions that restricted access and kept benefits low. If the amount of discretion had been enlarged or curbed, would the "right" decisions have been made earlier? Stated differently, should Congress have been more or less involved in establishing food stamp policy?

This is not an easy question to answer. In the early years of the program, when administrators had a great deal of discretion, they were responsible for the decisions that made the program much less accessible and generous than it should have been. Yet if Congress had made the decisions on the same issues, it is highly doubtful that the results would have been markedly different. When these policies were recognized as wrong, it was USDA and not the Congress that initiated reforms. In later years, however, Congress acted to keep administrators from implementing harsh and restrictive regulations that would have reduced assistance to those in need.

In sum, neither branch has been consistently wise in its conception of program policy. The rulemaking discretion available to USDA has not been used in a uniform fashion. As illustrated, it has been a tool for increasing participation as well as decreasing it. For its part, Congress has often shown itself to be incapable of making changes when changes have proved necessary. The conclusion that must be reached is that there is no general answer to the question of how much discretion has been best for food stamp policy making.

Possibly, this conclusion would be true for many different programs, and food stamps is more the rule than the exception. Still, even though the food stamp program has not provided a golden mean for optimal administrative discretion, it does offer some insight into the problems posed by scholars such as Lowi and Harris. To begin with, there have been no findings that would indicate that Congress deliberately ought to leave large grants of discretion in areas where it can make policy itself. As Charles Hyneman has noted, "First and fundamental, is the rule that Congress should specify in the statute every guide, every condition, every statement of principle that it knows in advance it wants to have applied in the situations that are expected to arise."[43] If Congress knows what it wants, then it should put its preferences into law rather than leaving them to an understanding or later intervention. If it is possible and practical, a policy decision ought to be made by the elected representatives of the people and not by administrators.

Since the case study of the food stamp program shows that Congress often does not know what policies it wants until *after* it passes legislation, Hyneman's rule leaves much ground uncovered. When Congress cannot agree upon an issue at the time it passes a law, would it be better, as Lowi implies, for administrators to refrain from setting their own policy? This inaction would force Congress to make subsequent decisions with highly specific standards of implementation. Or would it be more desirable to follow Harris's prescription? After Congress has gone as far as it chooses in its statutory decisions, administrators would have the freedom to formulate necessary policy without the meddling and intervention of congressmen.

It may be that Lowi is right in his contention that excessive delegation reflects the malaise of American politics. Lack of congressional direction may have resulted in interest groups becoming too influential in agency policy making. Unfortunately, Lowi's solutions are not practical.[44] The realities of congressional politics make it unlikely that the Congress can write statutes that contain explicit standards of implementation for all important areas of policy. Coalition building, the absence of consensus, and the impossibility of foreseeing the consequences of implementation all dictate that policy, and not just the details of legislation, will be set through rulemaking.

If broad discretion is a necessary reality, should Congress restrict its intervention, as Harris would like, in the regulation-writing process? Intervention is a means by which Congress gradually defines its intent and comes to understand the policy decisions that must be made. It is a messy process, blurring the lines of responsibility between Congress and agencies. Nevertheless, aggressive oversight and intervention represent the middle ground between two unworkable extremes. Perhaps the lesson from the food stamp program is this: Administrators must have the initial regulatory discretion to experiment, to adapt, to make mistakes—to find out what works and what does not—and Congress must faithfully review rulemaking and make its opinions known so that legislative intent is continually expressed.

Is aggressive oversight and intervention into rulemaking a realistic compromise between the need for discretion and the need for legislative specificity? Given the generally accepted view that Congress fails in its oversight role, it may not seem so. Yet the history of the food stamp program reveals a consistently high level of oversight and intervention for roughly fifteen years now. The legislative incentives for this behavior, stemming from interest group advocacy, the personal and political goals of congressmen and their staffs, and other sources, have proved to be quite powerful.

FOOD STAMPS AND WELFARE REFORM

It is not unusual for government programs to turn out to be something much more or something much less than they were originally intended to be. From a farm support and feeding plan to an in-kind negative income tax, the food stamp program has changed considerably since its initial conception. Richard Nathan has described this transformation of the food stamp program as "unintended welfare reform."[45]

Without question, the food stamp program has reformed the American welfare system. The development of the program has significantly affected the way the poor are treated in the United States. It serves the people who previously fell through the gaps of various categorical programs. It gives more money to the "welfare poor"—people who receive AFDC, social security, or other forms of assistance and still do not have enough to live decently on. The program's sliding income scale lessens the inequities of widely varying state AFDC benefit levels; the less a family receives in AFDC income, the more generous is its food stamp bonus. The food stamp program is an income floor for all Americans. In times of need, it is the one welfare program to which any person without a living income can turn.

Despite its early problems with participation, food stamps has become a highly accessible income maintenance program. In some months, roughly one out of every ten individuals in the populations has received food stamps. As many as one out of six Americans has been on food stamps at one time or another during a single year. With the Reagan administration's cuts in AFDC and other government programs, the food stamp program has become an even more important means of income maintenance.

The food stamp program has worked to reform the welfare system not only because it gives individuals the means to obtain more food, but also because it gives them more *cash*. Although the welfare benefit has always been issued in the form of coupons, the pricing structure leaves individuals with some money that they would otherwise have spent on food. The original purchase schedules were, of course, designed to prevent recipients from receiving this extra cash or "income transfer." When recipients actually paid close to their normal amount of food purchases for their stamps, there was little in the way of an income transfer. As the participation problem forced the addition of the shelter deduction, recipients began to spend less for their stamps. Other deductions and the general lowering of purchase prices in 1969 made the real cost of stamps even less related to the level of normal purchases. As a result, by 1977 the Congressional Budget Office estimated that only 57 percent of the food stamp bonus transfer was being spent on extra food. The other 43 percent was substituted for cash that would have been spent on food in the absence of the program.[46] Although many policy changes have been made since then, the program still provides recipients not only with more money for food but with more money period.

In 1964 probably few, if any, congressmen realized that they were creating a program that would develop into an in-kind guaranteed annual income with a hidden cash transfer. A Democrat who was on the House Agriculture Committee at the time later said, "Nobody contemplated that it would become a second welfare program." Yet, how unintended was this welfare reform accomplished through food stamps? Although no one in 1961 or 1964 could have easily envisioned what the food stamp program would become, advocacy on behalf of the program has been, since the very start, an effort at broader welfare reform. In the early 1960s there would have been little public support for the type of welfare reform that would give poor people more money. The basic thrust of the Kennedy administration's approach was to offer social services to the poor, not expanded cash assistance.[47] At the same time, the experiment with the food stamp pilot projects was an acknowledgement that some people did not have enough money for the bare necessities of life. *The solution was to call welfare reform "hunger."*

The American public has not grown any more supportive of large-scale welfare reform since the beginnings of the food stamp program. Carter's guaranteed annual income proposal fared worse in Congress than Nixon's Family Assistance Plan. The Reagan administration is not interested in reforming the system through a negative income tax.[48] Aside from Reagan's philosophical objections, it does not seem possible to create such a system with a reasonable eligibility line that would not be more, rather than less, costly.

Of major significance to the food stamp program is the Reagan administration's efforts to target budget cuts at the working poor.[49] By reducing the eligibility line and the earned income deduction, the administration may actually reduce the incentive of some recipients to work. This represents a dramatic change of strategy in dealing with the poor. In years past, the AFDC and food stamp programs have been reformed to encourage recipients to take part-time or low-paying jobs as the first step toward working themselves off of welfare. The changes in the deductions and eligibility rules for AFDC, food stamps, and Medicaid make it more difficult for many people to accept low-paying or part-time jobs because of the accompanying loss of benefits.

For liberal supporters of food stamps, the Reagan era is a time of simply trying to minimize program budget cuts. When a more sympathetic administration comes to power, there will surely be efforts to relax at least some of the Reagan retrenchments. A more ambitious step for liberals would be to push for enactment of a "cash out" of food stamps so that participants would receive money instead of coupons. So long as coupons are given out rather than cash, the program will always have a demeaning aspect.[50] When stamps are used at the checkout counter, they are a nonverbal admission to any observer that the users are poor, unemployed, or otherwise incapable of providing for themselves and their families. Not only does the coupon system stigmatize those who use it, but it also inhibits some from participating in the program because of the embarrassment. It will be difficult for liberals to win passage of such a reform, however, because conservatives will see it as the first step toward a negative income tax.

Whatever its shortcomings, the food stamp program is a success. It is a success because it has improved the quality of people's lives.[51] Money for food may not buy happiness, but it can alleviate misery.

CONCLUSION

Since the first pilot projects opened in 1961, there have been six major reforms of the food stamp program. First, the shelter deduction took effect in 1963. Second and third, benefits were raised to the level of the economy food plan and purchase prices were lowered in 1969. The fourth reform was the nationalized eligibility line included in the 1970 legislation. Fifth, Congress voted to eliminate the purchase price for all families. Sixth, and finally, the Reagan administration's fiscal year 1982 budget cuts resulted in a trimming of benefits through a number of related actions. Of these six reforms, three were initiated through regulation and three through statute. But this simple division of major decisions does not do justice to the complex patterns of legislative-agency interaction that have been responsible for food stamp policy. Food stamp rulemaking can only be understood as part of both the legislative and the administrative process. Food stamp legislation has always embodied responses to administrative regulations.⟩

The enormous impact of administrative guidelines on the development of food stamp policy demonstrates the significance of regulations in the welfare and social services area. For too long the study of administrative rulemaking has concentrated on economic regulatory agencies. Nothing is more deserving of our attention than the way government treats society's underclass. The typical food stamp recipient is a child, an old person, or an individual unable to find work.

Although patterns of congressional-agency relations must differ greatly from one policy field to another, the underlying problem of the delegation of authority remains the same. The case of the food stamp program shows that it is extremely difficult to specify the optimal mix of congressional responsibility and administrative discretion. If the most desirable degree of discretion must stand as indeterminate, it is all the more important that the process of writing regulations warrants the freedom that imprecise grants of discretion allow. In the past, the writing of food stamp regulations has not been a model of an open and accessible administrative process. Despite the exemption for welfare grants under the Administrative Procedure Act, there is no compelling reason why the program rules were allowed to escape notice and comment during the early years. The Food and Nutrition Service has improved the way food stamp regulations are written, but for too many years of the program's existence administrators have been hostile and inaccessible to representatives of their clients.

For Americans to have confidence in and respect for their government, they must believe they have meaningful ways of influencing it. A bureaucracy that appears to be inpenetrable and that is perceived to write regulations through incomprehensible procedures will breed contempt and disrespect no matter how wise its decisions.[52] If agency administrators are to be truly responsive to all their clients, they must ensure that citizen participation programs present real opportunities to influence rulemaking. Administrators must also be accessible to interest group representatives of varying ideological stripes and not just to those who agree with them.

For its part, Congress must continue to scrutinize the regulatory activities of FNS. Since no consistent standard of administrative responsibility has guided food stamp officials and no level of discretion has been found to be optimal, Congress must actively oversee agency policy making to ensure that its intent is carried out. Ultimately, Congress is responsible for FNS policies, either through its apathy or through its conscious affirmation, refinement, or rejection of agency regulations.

Epilogue

AGAIN, HUNGER

OF ALL THE MAJOR poverty-related problems that the federal government attacked during the 1960s, hunger probably came the closest to being solved.[1] Indeed, in less than twenty years food stamps and other nutrition programs seemingly made hunger a concern of the past. Thus it is a bitter irony that in the 1980s hunger is again a serious national problem.

The situation is by no means comparable to the years before food stamps and various child nutrition programs were instituted. The progress made since then remains impressive. Still, some preliminary statistical evidence from medical research reports shows that hunger has already begun to take its toll on the health of the nation's poor.[2] The most compelling and visible evidence of hunger, however, is to be found in the faces of the poor who line up outside of food banks and soup kitchens. They are faces of want and deprivation—faces that seem out of place in our modern post-industrial society. As with earlier periods of controversy over hunger, the media have played a crucial role. Television news stories especially, with their footage of humbled people going through food banks, have helped to put hunger back on the political agenda.

The rising incidence of hunger and malnutrition springs from two sources. The first is the severe recession that gripped the country from the summer of 1981 until an apparent recovery began in the spring of 1983. With the unemployment rate pushed close to 11 percent and receding only slowly, many people have been forced to a marginal existence for the first time in their lives. Large numbers of families have had to struggle to keep enough food on the table.

The second reason for the growing hunger problem is the reduction of funding levels for the government's nutrition programs. These cuts, enacted by Congress at the urging of the Reagan administration,

149

have restricted eligibility and reduced benefits. The Reagan administration's rhetoric aside, the savings have not been accomplished
largely through administrative belt-tightening or by eliminating fraud
and waste. In fiscal year 1982, over $3 billion was cut from govern-
ment nutrition programs. As noted earlier, the food stamp program
alone has lost approximately $11 billion for fiscal years 1982–1985
from the cuts made in 1981 and 1982. Conservatives argue that spending cuts merely slow the growth of a runaway program. Inevitably
though, cuts in food stamps mean tighter family budgets and less
money for food.

When the economy fully heals from the recession, the hunger
problem will disappear for many, and it may recede from the public's
eye as well. Yet it is important to remember that nearly 80 percent of
all food stamp recipients are children, single parents, senior citizens,
and the disabled. For those individuals and families largely outside
the job market, the budget cuts will continue to hurt. It is critical
that scholars and government policy analysts closely monitor the long-
term consequences of the reductions in nutrition spending on all the
target populations.

The more immediate response to the hunger issue by the federal
government, state and local governments, and private organizations
has been to offer emergency assistance through food banks. They provide the poor with direct gifts of food that can supplement other forms
of assistance (if any). Much of the donated food comes from the federal
government, which takes surplus commodities out of storage and ships
them to local agencies to distribute to the needy.

Despite their good intentions, food banks fall short for a variety of
reasons. To begin with, there is no coherent distribution system. The
location of food banks is a hit-or-miss proposition. And where they are
accessible, they often have little to offer. Some recipients go away with
only a five-pound block of American cheese. Other food banks have
been able to offer at least a small bag of canned goods, cheese, butter,
and the like.

Food banks strip individuals of their dignity by making them go to
the modern-day equivalent of a poorhouse to ask for a handout. Many
people, of course, swallow their pride and take advantage of the available food. They do so because they are desperate or feel that they must
put their children's health ahead of their own personal dignity. Others,
though, choose to endure hunger rather than submit to the humiliation
of waiting in line for charity.

150

Handouts are not the most appropriate way of addressing the hunger problem. It was the failure of the commodity distribution program, of course, that led to the creation of the food stamp program in 1961. Still, it is difficult to convince people that food banks are a step backwards because they seem to combine humanitarianism with good common sense. What can be wrong with taking surplus food out of warehouses and putting it into the mouths of the hungry? What is wrong is that food banks distract attention away from programs that work and thus reduce the pressure on government to stop cutting those same programs.

Although the Reagan administration has acknowledged the need for food assistance by backing legislation to expand distribution of commodities, it nonetheless continues to push for more cuts in nutrition programs. In its budget proposal to the Congress for fiscal year 1984, the administration recommended that about $1.5 billion be slashed from nutrition, the bulk of it ($1.1 billion) to be taken from food stamps. Secretary of Agriculture John Block defended the budget reduction for food stamps by claiming that the changes were designed primarily to "improve our efficiency in administering the program."[3] If enacted, the savings would come mostly from reducing the amount of allowable income deductions and from shifting costs to the states by penalizing them for errors made by the caseworkers who determine benefits.

At this writing it seems doubtful that the Congress will allow any significant food stamps cuts in its final 1984 budget. The House passed a budget resolution that called for a $900 million increase in food stamps. The Senate is sure to be less generous, but a final funding level that represents no cuts or a small increase seems likely. Yet the fact that the administration is still able to propose such funding cuts attests to continuing shallow public support for nutrition programs. Food stamps has still not escaped the negative image that has so hurt it in recent years. Nevertheless, the growing awareness of the hunger problem has enabled supporters in the Congress to blunt efforts to cut nutrition even further.

The future for food stamps and other nutrition programs remains troublesome. Although there is currently little sentiment in the Congress or among the American people for more overall cuts in domestic spending, the budget deficits projected for coming years will continue to put pressure on large welfare programs like food stamps. Until the gap between revenues and expenditures is closed, it will be extremely difficult for program backers to win significant increases in food stamp spending. Furthermore, the hunger lobby and sympathizers in Congress have yet to convince the American public that the recent cuts are directly responsible for increased hunger and malnutrition.

The national commitment to eradicate hunger has not come to an end, but it has weakened. It is the task once again of those who support nutrition programs to convince the American public that when it comes to food for the hungry, it is government's responsibility to be thy brother's keeper.

NOTES

Introduction

1. For a thorough analysis of all the different parts of the Administrative Procedure Act, see Kenneth Culp Davis, *Administrative Law*, 6th ed. (St. Paul: West, 1977), pp. 221–269.

2. Louis Fisher, *President and Congress* (New York: Free Press, 1972), pp. 55–77; Sotirios A. Barber, *The Constitution and the Delegation of Congressional Power* (Chicago: Unibersity of Chicago Press, 1975).

3. James O. Freedman, *Crisis and Legitimacy* (New York: Cambridge University Press, 1978).

4. The literature on regulation is voluminous and cannot be entirely cited here. For some of the early classics, see Marver H. Bernstein, *Regulating Business by Independent Commission* (Princeton: Princeton University Press, 1955); Walter Gellhorn, *Federal Administrative Proceedings* (Baltimore: Johns Hopkins University Press, 1941); James M. Landis, *The Administrative Process* (New Haven: Yale University Press, 1938); and Avery Leiserson, *Administrative Regulation* (Chicago: University of Chicago Press, 1942).

5. For a comprehensive overview of recent research, see Barry M. Mitnick, *The Political Economy of Regulation: Creating, Designing, and Removing Regulatory Forms* (New York: Columbia University Press, 1980).

6. Allen Schick, "Congress and the Details of Administration," *Public Administration Review* 36 (September-October 1976):516–528.

7. See Hans A. Linde and George Bunn, *Legislative and Administrative Processes* (Mineola, N.Y.: Foundation Press, 1976), pp. 363–389.

8. Legislative intervention into such agency procedures as adjudication and rate making appears, however, to be far less common.

9. David R. Mayhew, *Congress: The Electoral Connection* (New Haven: Yale University Press, 1974).

10. See Joel D. Aberbach, "The Development of Oversight in the United States Congress: Concepts and Analysis," paper delivered at the annual meeting of the American Political Science Association, Washington, D.C., September 1977. In

his major study of oversight, Morris Ogul allows for intervention as oversight but does not cover it in any detail; see Ogul, *Congress Oversees the Bureaucracy* (Pittsburgh: University of Pittsburgh Press, 1976).

11. Harry C. Boyte, *The Backyard Revolution* (Philadelphia: Temple University Press, 1980).

12. Samuel P. Huntington, "The Democratic Distemper," *Public Interest* 41 (Fall 1975):9–38.

13. D. Stephen Cupps, "Emerging Problems of Citizen Participation," *Public Administration Review* 37 (September-October 1977):478–487; Jeffrey M. Berry, "Public Interest Vs. Party System," *Society* 17 (May-June 1980):42–48; David Cohen, "Future Directions for the Public Interest Movement," *Citizen Participation* 3 (March-April 1982):3ff.

14. Mancur Olson, Jr., *The Logic of Collective Action* (New York: Schocken, 1968).

15. Jeffrey M. Berry, *Lobbying for the People* (Princeton: Princeton University Press, 1977), pp. 6–11.

16. See Stuart Langton, ed., *Citizen Participation in America* (Lexington, Mass.: D. C. Heath, 1978); Symposium on Citizen Participation in Public Policy, *Journal of Applied Behavioral Science* 17 (October 1981).

17. See, generally, Douglass Cater, *Power in Washington* (New York: Random House, 1964); J. Leiper Freeman, *The Political Process*, 2nd ed. (New York: Random House, 1965); Roger H. Davidson, "Breaking Up Those 'Cozy Triangles': An Impossible Dream?" in Susan Welch and John G. Peters, eds., *Legislative Reform and Public Policy* (New York: Praeger, 1977), pp. 30–53.

18. Lawrence C. Dodd and Richard L. Schott, *Congress and the Administrative State* (New York: Wiley, 1979), p. 103.

19. Hugh Heclo, "Issue Networks and the Executive Establishment," in Anthony King, ed., *The New American Political System* (Washington, D.C.: American Enterprise Institute, 1978), pp. 87–124.

20. Ibid., p. 102.

21. Ibid., p. 104.

22. Dodd and Schott, *Congress and the Administrative State*, p. 173.

23. See Theodore J. Lowi, "American Business, Public Policy, Case Studies, and Political Theory," *World Politics* 16 (July 1964):677–715; Michael Hayes, *Lobbyists and Legislators* (New Brunswick, N.J.: Rutgers University Press, 1981).

24. Linde and Bunn, *Legislative and Administrative Processes*.

25. Theodore J. Lowi, *The End of Liberalism* (New York: Norton, 1969).

26. Davis, *Administrative Law*, p. 35. Within the framework of clear legislative intent as to how an agency should solve major problems, Davis sees tremendous value in the rulemaking process. See his *Discretionary Justice* (Baton Rouge: Louisiana State University Press, 1969).

27. James Q. Wilson, "The Rise of the Bureaucratic State," *Public Interest* 41 (Fall 1975):103.

28. Joseph P. Harris, *Congressional Control of Administration* (Washington, D.C.: Brookings Institution, 1964), p. 2.

29. Herbert Kaufman, "Fear of Bureaucracy: A Raging Pandemic," *Public Administration Review* 41 (January-February 1981):3.

30. Carl J. Friedrich, "Public Policy and the Nature of Administrative Responsibility," *Public Policy* 1 (1940):3–24.

31. Herman Finer, "Administrative Responsibility in Democratic Government," *Public Administration Review* 1 (Summer 1941):335–350.

32. The standards for evaluating the regulations in relation to this question are discussed in Chapter 6.

33. The guidelines of the early years were, in effect, the program regulations, though they lacked the actual legal standing. Under the exemption for welfare grants in the Administrative Procedure Act, they did not have to be put through notice and comment. Later, as will be shown, they were put through notice and comment and became part of the *Code of Federal Regulations*.

34. See, generally, Jeffrey M. Berry, "Food Stamps: The Recurring Issues," in Don Hadwiger and William Browne, eds., *The New Politics of Food* (Lexington, Mass.: D. C. Heath, 1978), pp. 151–162; Kenneth W. Clarkson, *Food Stamps and Nutrition* (Washington, D.C.: American Enterprise Institute, 1975); *Food Stamp Act of 1976*, H. Rept. 1460, 94 Cong., 2 sess., 1976, pp. 390–495; Congressional Budget Office, *The Food Stamp Program: Income or Food Supplementation?*, January 1977; Maurice MacDonald, *Food, Stamps, and Income Maintenance* (New York: Academic Press, 1977); Richard P. Nathan, "Food Stamps and Welfare Reform, *Policy Analysis* 2 (Winter 1976):61–70; Gilbert Y. Steiner, *The State of Welfare* (Washington, D.C.: Brookings Institution, 1971), pp. 191–236.

35. Adam Clymer, "Public Prefers a Balanced Budget to Large Cut in Taxes, Poll Shows," *New York Times*, February 3, 1981.

Chapter 1. A Second Chance for Food Stamps

1. The best historical account of the program prior to its revival in 1961 is contained in *Food Stamp Act of 1976*, H. Rept. 1460, 94 Cong., 2 sess., 1976, pp. 390–495.

2. Ibid., p. 395.

3. Norman Leon Gold, A. C. Hoffman, and Frederick V. Waugh, "Economic Analysis of the Food Stamp Plan," USDA, Bureau of Agricultural Economics and the Surplus Marketing Administration, 1940.

4. USDA, "An Analysis of Food Stamp Plans," 1957, History Group Files.

5. An account of the legislative maneuvering over food stamps in the late

1950s is contained in Randall B. Ripley, "Legislative Bargaining and the Food Stamp Act, 1964," in Frederic N. Cleaveland and Associates, *Congress and Urban Problems* (Washington, D.C.: Brookings Institution, 1969), pp. 281–288.

6. *Food Stamp Plans*, hearings before the House Committee on Agriculture, 85 Cong., 1 sess., 1959, p. 14.

7. Ibid., p. 15.

8. See USDA, "Proposed Pilot Food Stamp Programs," n.d. (but sometime around December 1960–January 1961), History Group Files; Faith Clark, "Background Statement on Derivation of Cost of 'Nutritious Economy Diet' Proposed for Pilot Food Stamp Program," February 13, 1961, History Group Files.

9. *Federal Register*, May 13, 1961, pp. 4137–4440. Over time, as will be shown, more and more food stamp guidelines appeared in the *Federal Register*. The same guidelines that escaped the process of notice and comment at this point were later put through it, although not for almost ten years in many cases.
  Also in May 1961, a decision was made to change the statutory authorization of the program. Since Congresswoman Sullivan's plan (1959) dealt only with surplus foods, it would not suffice for the "free market" plan designed by Davis, Kelley, and Vanneman. Instead, they used a 1935 amendment to the Agricultural Adjustment Act as their basis of authority for the program. This provision, Section 32, empowered the secretary of agriculture to set up programs to encourage domestic consumption of food outside the normal channels of trade.

10. In accordance with President Kennedy's wishes, most of the first group of pilot projects opened in poor mining regions. The other projects areas were: Floyd County, Kentucky; the Virginia-Hibbing-Nashwauk area of Minnesota; Silver Bow County, Montana; San Miguel County, New Mexico; Fayette County, Pennsylvania; Franklin County, Illinois; and Detroit, Michigan.

11. Tom Wicker, "First Food Given in Stamp Project," *New York Times*, May 30, 1961.

12. "JFK Food Stamps a Success in Initial Fayette County Test," *Pittsburgh Press*, July 16, 1961.

13. USDA, Consumer and Marketing Service, Food Stamp Division, "The Food Stamp Program: An Initial Evaluation of the Pilot Projects," April 1962. See also USDA, Economic Research Service, Marketing Economics Division, "Effects of the Pilot Food Stamp Program on Retail Food Store Sales," Agricultural Economic Report no. 8, April 1962; USDA Economic Research Service and Agricultural Research Service, "Food Consumption and Dietary Levels Under the Pilot Food Stamp Program," Agricultural Economic Report no. 9, June 1962. Later research would throw doubt on the finding that the diet of program participants actually improved in terms of their intake of key nutrients. See J. Patrick Madden and Marion D. Yoder, *Food Stamp and Commodity Distribution in Rural Areas of Central Pennsylvania* (University Park: Pennsylvania State University, 1972); Sylvia Lane, "Food Distribution and Food Stamp Program Effects on Food Consumption and Nutritional 'Achievement' of Low Income Persons in Kern County, California," *American Journal of Agricultural Economics* 60 (February 1978):108–116.

14. "The Food Stamp Program: An Initial Evaluation of the Pilot Projects," pp. 13–15.

15. Julius Duscha of the *Washington Post* was one of the few who recognized the importance of the participation problem in Detroit. See his articles, "New Food Stamp Plan Causing Some Hardship in Detroit Area," *Washington Post*, December 10, 1961, and "Food Stamp Plan Cuts Total of Aid Applicants," *Washington Post*, December 11, 1961. In contrast to Duscha's stories, see the more optimistic reporting of Damon Stetson, "Detroit Applauds Food Stamp Plan," *New York Times*, December 10, 1961.

16. *Amend the Food Stamp Act of 1964*, hearings before the House Committee on Agriculture, 90 Cong, 2 sess., 1968, p. 28.

17. For example, a family with an income of $100 and shelter costs of $62 a month would have an adjusted income of $68 after the shelter deduction ($100 minus the $32 excess over 30 percent of gross income). This meant that the family would only have to pay $28 for stamps (the charge for families with incomes of $68) rather than $44 (the charge for families with incomes of $100). Unfortunately, because of the sliding scale for allotments as well, the amount of stamps received in return would be reduced from $78 to $66. The net amount of bonus stamps would, however, increase from $34 to $38. These computations are derived from the 1964 basis of issuance tables for northern states.

18. Mandatory payroll deductions, such as income tax or social security, were always excluded from a family's income. For those who were employed, take-home pay, not gross income, was used in figuring out food stamp income.

19. *Extend the Food Stamp Act of 1964 and Amend the Child Nutrition Act of 1966*, hearings before the House Committee on Agriculture, 90 Cong., 1 sess., 1967, p. 80.

20. Julius Duscha, "House Unit Kills Food Stamp Bill," *Washington Post*, February 4, 1964.

21. Ripley, "Legislative Bargaining and the Food Stamp Act, 1964," pp. 296–300.

22. Ibid. Ripley's study is an excellent and detailed account of the passage of the food stamp bill.

23. For an overview of how the structure of the congressional system facilitates logrolling, see David R. Mayhew, *Congress: The Electoral Connection* (New Haven: Yale University Press, 1974).

24. Ripley, "Legislative Bargaining and the Food Stamp Act, 1964," p. 300.

25. P. L. 88–525.

26. "Remarks of the President on the Occasion of the Signing of the Food Stamp Act of 1964," White House press release, August 31, 1964, LBJ files.

27. Kenneth G. Slocum, "Food Stamp Program Improves Diet for Many, Wins Wide Acceptance," *Wall Street Journal*, September 30, 1966.

28. A useful analysis of the House Agriculture Committee around this time is

Charles O. Jones, "Representation in Congress: The Case of the House Agriculture Committee," *American Political Science Review* 55 (June 1961):358–367.

Chapter 2. Hunger Becomes an Issue

1. For an evaluation of what was accomplished by the Great Society, see Sar A. Levitan and Robert Taggart, *The Promise of Greatness* (Cambridge, Mass.: Harvard University Press, 1976).

2. *Poverty, Malnutrition, and Federal Food Assistance Programs: A Statistical Summary*, prepared by the Select Committee on Nutrition and Human Needs, 91 Cong., 1 sess., 1969, pp. 33–34.

3. Ibid.

4. *Nutrition and Human Needs, Part 2—USDA, HEW and OEO Officials*, hearings before the Select Committee on Nutrition and Human Needs, 91 Cong., 1 sess., 1969, pp. 332–333.

5. Gilbert Y. Steiner, *The State of Welfare* (Washington, D.C.: Brookings Institution, 1971), p. 214.

6. Robert Reese and Sadye Adelson, "Preliminary Report, Special Survey of Needy Families not Participating in the Food Stamp Program, St. Louis, Missouri, May-June 1964," September 15, 1964, History Group Files. A later draft is reprinted in *Nutrition and Human Needs, Part 2*, pp. 397–427.

7. On the process of agenda building, see Roger W. Cobb and Charles D. Elder, *Participation in American Politics: The Dynamics of Agenda Building* (Boston: Allyn and Bacon, 1972).

8. As quoted in Nick Kotz, *Let Them Eat Promises* (1969; rpt. Garden City, N.Y.: Anchor Books, 1971), p. 5.

9. Joseph A. Loftus, "Clark and Kennedy Visit the Poor of Mississippi," *New York Times*, April 12, 1967; "No Escalation," *Time*, April 21, 1967, p. 24.

10. Kotz, *Let Them Eat Promises*, pp. 8–9.

11. Joint prepared statement of Joseph Brenner et al, *Hunger and Malnutrition in America*, hearings before the Subcommittee on Employment, Manpower, and Poverty of the Senate Committee on Labor and Public Welfare, 90 Cong., 1 sess., 1967, p. 46.

12. William Chapman, "Hunger in Mississippi," reprinted in *Hunger and Malnutrition in America*, pp. 270–272.

13. "Lord I'm Hungry," in ibid., pp. 277–278.

14. Richard L. Strout, "Living in a Tar-Paper Shack," in ibid., pp. 274–276.

15. Citizens' Board of Inquiry, *Hunger U.S.A.* (Washington, D.C.: New Community Press, 1968).

16. The transcript of the show is reprinted in *Hunger and Malnutrition in the*

United States, hearings before the Subcommittee on Employment, Manpower, and Poverty of the Senate Labor and Public Welfare Committee, 90 Cong., 2 sess., 1968, pp. 55–64.

17. Kotz, *Let Them Eat Promises.*

18. One southern politician who stood out for his support of a stronger federal role in alleviating hunger was Senator Ernest Hollings (D.–S.C.). When Hollings heard that the Clark subcommittee was planning to hold hunger hearings in South Carolina, he angrily called Bobby Kennedy and told him that if the subcommittee went to South Carolina, he, Hollings, would start an investigation of hunger in Harlem in Kennedy's home state of New York. Hollings told Kennedy that after his 1968 reelection campaign he would do his own investigation of hunger in South Carolina. He kept his word, and the antihunger forces received a valuable ally: a respected white, southern politician who admitted there were large numbers of hungry people in his own state. See Ernest F. Hollings, *The Case Against Hunger* (New York: Cowles, 1970), pp. 32–42.

19. Public interest groups were forming on many policy issues at this time. See Jeffrey M. Berry, "On the Origins of Public Interest Groups: A Test of Two Theories," *Polity* 10 (Spring 1978):379–397.

20. See, generally, Francis Fox Piven and Richard Cloward, *Poor People's Movements* (New York: Pantheon, 1978).

21. Memorandum from DeVier Pierson to President Johnson, June 12, 1968, p. 1, LBJ Files.

22. See John W. Kingdon, *Congressmen's Voting Decisions* (New York: Harper and Row, 1973); David R. Mayhew, *Congress: The Electoral Connection* (New Haven: Yale University Press, 1974); Warren E. Miller and Donald E. Stokes, "Constituency Influence in Congress," *American Political Science Review* 57 (March 1963):45–56.

23. Sympathy for the food stamp program was not aided by a Republican resurgence in the 1966 congressional elections. The GOP picked up forty-seven House seats. Although many of these were normally Republican seats that had fallen to the Democrats in the Johnson landslide over Barry Goldwater, the results of the election were widely interpreted as a backlash of sorts against the social programs of the Great Society.

24. Memorandum from Orville Freeman to President Johnson, n.d. (but sometime in spring 1968), p. 2, LBJ Files.

25. At one point, during one of the most successful and productive periods of the committee's history, a staffer offered the *New York Times's* Washington bureau exclusive use of some sensitive documents leaked to the committee. The price the *Times* would have to pay was a promise to put the story to be written from the documents on page one. The *Times* reporter asked the New York headquarters for permission to make the deal. The story ran on page one.

26. Steiner, *The State of Welfare,* p. 236.

27. "The Food Stamp Program: A Position Paper on the Minimum Purchase Re-

quirements," memorandum from Isabelle Kelley to Rodney Leonard, February 15, 1967, p. 7, History Group Files (Rod Leonard Files).

28. Memorandum from Rodney Leonard to Orville Freeman, February 27, 1967, p. 1, History Group Files (Rod Leonard Files).

29. Memorandum from Ken Birkhead to Orville Freeman, April 17, 1967, p. 1, History Group Files (Orville Freeman Files). The Northern Minimum was $4.00, but the controversy surrounded the $2.00 Southern minimum.

30. Memorandum from Joseph Califano to President Johnson, April 17, 1967, LBJ Files.

31. See "Food Aid Program Revamped by U.S.," New York Times, June 27, 1967; Food Stamp Instruction 67–58 (revised), USDA. Another announcement stated that USDA was starting a program through its local Technical Action Panels that would seek out nonparticipants.

32. Memorandum from Joseph Califano to President Johnson, June 28, 1968; memorandum from Califano to Johnson, July 1, 1968; memorandum from Califano to Johnson, July 10, 1968, LBJ Files.

33. Steiner, The State of Welfare, p. 224.

34. Mayhew, Congress: The Electoral Connection, p. 125, and generally, pp. 52–61, 110–40. Mayhew also notes that there is little to be gained for intervention on income transfer programs: "What distinguishes American transfer programs is not that they are 'redistributive' . . . but that they offer legislators no particularized benefits. Who gets a check of what size is clearly prescribed by law, so congressmen get no credit for the handing out of individual checks" (pp. 136–137).

Chapter 3. Reform through Regulation

1. Weekly Compilation of Presidential Documents, February 10, 1969, p. 212.

2. "Urban Affairs Council Materials on Hunger and Malnutrition," staff memorandum, May 1, 1969. Reprinted in Nutrition and Human Needs, Part 8—The Nixon Administration Program, hearings before the Select Committee on Nutrition and Human Needs, 91 Cong., 1 sess., 1969, pp. 2566–2567.

3. Ibid., p. 2567.

4. On the consequences of this distrust, see Richard P. Nathan, The Plot That Failed (New York: John Wiley, 1975).

5. Nutrition and Human Needs, Part 8, pp. 2565–2615.

6. Daniel P. Moynihan, The Politics of a Guaranteed Income (New York: Vintage, 1973), p. 121.

7. Using a transcript of this meeting, Nick Kotz quotes Nixon as responding to one of Hardin's pleas as follows: "You can say that this administration will have the first complete, far reaching attack on hunger in history. Use all the rhetoric, so long as it doesn't cost any money." Kotz, Let Them Eat Promises

(1969; rpt. Garden City, N.Y.: Anchor Books, 1971), p. 200. Kotz believed that the president meant what he said: There would be no big spending proposal for food stamps. This interpretation is contradicted by one interviewee, a participant at the meeting, who claimed the president was making a joke when he said, "Use all the rhetoric, so long as it doesn't cost any money." Daniel Moynihan makes the same case, writing that Nixon's answer was intended, and understood, as a joke; Moynihan, *The Politics of a Guaranteed Income*, p. 122. A slightly different interpretation is offered by another interviewee (also interviewed by Kotz), who said that the president really was making a commitment, he just did not want to put a price tag on it yet.

8. Wishing to avoid any controversy over the normal purchase requirement of the food stamp law, Hardin used Section 32 money to fund two projects in South Carolina; see Chapter 1, note 9. The free stamps went to families with incomes of less than thirty dollars a month, who previously had paid fifty cents per person for their stamps.

9. See Spencer Rich, "Cabinet Plan Urged Bigger Hunger Fund," *Washington Post*, May 3, 1969.

10. Kenneth Schlossberg concludes that it was Clifford Hardin who changed Nixon's mind: "The day before he was scheduled to appear, Hardin made a last ditch, personal plea to Nixon. Nixon changed his mind, giving Hardin the go ahead. . . ." Schlossberg, "Funny Money Is Serious," *New York Times Magazine*, September 28, 1975, p. 13.

11. Moynihan, *Politics of a Guaranteed Income*, p. 124.

12. See Robert Walters, "Food Feud at White House Surfaces at Hunger Meeting," *Washington Star*, December 4, 1969.

13. The cost of the economy food plan had risen through inflation to $106 a month for a family of four by the time these reforms were implemented. For a description of the development of a USDA diet plan, see *Food Stamp Act of 1976*, H. Rept. 1460, 94 Cong., 2 sess., 1976, pp. 210–229.

14. The skillful committee leader knows not only when to lead but also when to be led. See John Manley's excellent study of Wilbur Mills's leadership of the House Ways and Means Committee, *The Politics of Finance* (Boston: Little, Brown, 1970).

15. The history of FAP has been detailed in M. Kenneth Bowler, *The Nixon Guaranteed Annual Income Proposal* (Cambridge, Mass.: Ballinger, 1974); Vincent J. Burke and Vee Burke, *Nixon's Good Deed* (New York: Columbia University Press, 1974); Moynihan, *Politics of a Guaranteed Income*.

16. See Burke and Burke, *Nixon's Good Deed*, pp. 120–123.

17. Don Oberdorfer, "Welfare Plan Hit on Cut in Food Stamps," *Washington Post*, August 12, 1969. For documentation on the effect of the initial FAP proposal on welfare recipients, see *Poverty, Malnutrition, and Federal Food Assistance Programs: A Statistical Summary*, prepared by the Select Committee on Nutrition and Human Needs, 91 Cong., 1 sess., 1969, pp. 43–56. See also, *Nutrition and Human Needs, Part 12—Welfare Reform and Food Stamps*, hear-

ings before the Senate Select Committee on Nutrition and Human Needs, 91 Cong., 1 sess., 1969.

18. Burke and Burke, *Nixon's Good Deed*, p. 177.

19. Richard P. Nathan, "The Case for Incrementalism," *City Almanac* 11 (December 1976):10.

20. P.L. 91–671.

21. For an analysis of this exemption, see Kenneth Culp Davis, *Administrative Law*, 6th ed. (St. Paul: West, 1977), pp. 241–247.

22. On the growth and development of the public interest law movement, see Robert L. Rabin, "Lawyers for Social Change: Perspectives on Public Interest Law," *Stanford Law Review* 28 (January 1976):207–261; Burton Weisbrod, *Public Interest Law* (Berkeley: University of California Press, 1978).

23. Although this figure constituted a food stamp poverty line, it was not the line generally referred to as the government's official poverty index. The government's general or Office of Management and Budget (OMB) poverty line, developed by Mollie Orshansky of HEW in 1964, was set at 3.0 times the level of the economy food plan. In 1971 the OMB line was $4,137. See Robert D. Plotnick and Felicity Skidmore, *Progress Against Poverty* (New York: Academic Press, 1975), pp. 31–46.

24. A subsequent study showed that 60 to 70 percent of all recipients took advantage of the shelter deduction. Janice Peskin, "The Shelter Deduction in the Food Stamp Program," HEW, Office of Income Security Policy, Technical Analysis Paper no. 6, August, 1975, p. 8.

25. For Pollack's testimony on these and other issues, see *Nutrition and Human Needs, 1971, Part 3—Food Stamp Regulations*, hearings before the Senate Select Committee on Nutrition and Human Needs, 92 Cong., 1 sess, 1971, pp. 759–793.

26. Ibid., pp. 982–988.

27. *Federal Register*, July 29, 1971, pp. 14102–14120.

28. See "Pennsylvania, New York Sue USDA on New Food Stamp Rules; Protest Mounts Against Regulations," *CNI Weekly Report*, January 6, 1972, pp. 1–2; "Food Stamp Conference Asks Moratorium on New Regulations; 14 States Sign Resolution," *CNI Weekly Report*, January 13, 1972, pp. 1–2.

29. Jack Rosenthal, "10% Is Impounded in Food Stamp Aid," *New York Times*, January 12, 1972.

30. On the presidency and impoundments, see Louis Fisher, *Presidential Spending Power* (Princeton: Princeton University Press, 1975), pp. 147–201.

31. *Federal Register*, January 26, 1972, p. 1180. See also "Nixon Administration Backs Down on Food Stamp Benefit Tables; Congress, Governors Win Victory," *CNI Weekly Report*, January 20, 1972, pp. 1–2.

32. The hunger lobby also worked on a few other, minor issues. The regulations contained a restrictive definition of what constituted a legitimate food stamp

household. This followed from congressional intent to render hippie communes ineligible for the program. Although hunger lobbyists were unable to get the definition relaxed in the regulations, they later successfully challenged it in court. The regulations also restricted to $1,500 the amount of liquid assets a family could have and still be eligible for the program. The hunger lobby was not able to get this amount liberalized. See *Nutrition and Human Needs, 1971, Part 3.*

Chapter 4. Cutting Back on Food Stamps

1. *Agriculture-Environmental and Consumer Protection Appropriations for 1972*, hearings before a subcommittee of the House Committee on Appropriations, 92 Cong., 1 sess., 1971, part 4, p. 114.

2. *Anderson v. Butz*, Civil No. 5–75–401.

3. For a transcript of Simon's speech and a rebuttal to the charges, see *Food Stamps: The Statement of Hon. William E. Simon, Secretary of the Treasury, With a Staff Analysis*, prepared by the Senate Select Committee on Nutrition and Human Needs, 94 Cong., 1 sess., 1975. See also, *The Food Stamp Controversy of 1975: Background Materials*, prepared by the Senate Select Committee on Nutrition and Human Needs, 94 Cong., 1 sess., 1975.

4. See Michael Satchell's articles, "U.S. Food Stamp Program Error—$797 Million?" *Washington Star*; "What They Don't Tell About Food Stamp Estimates—'Twenty-Four Thousandths of 1 Percent Was a Bit Low,'" *Washington Star*, October 29, 1975; and "Program Mushroomed . . . From Aid for the Very Poor—A Vital Income Source for 1 in Every 11 Americans," *Washington Star*, October 30, 1975.

5. Trevor Armbrister, "Time to Clean Up the Food Stamp Mess," *Reader's Digest*, July 1975, p. 64.

6. "Food Stamps: Out of Control?" *U.S. News and World Report*, September 1, 1975, p. 12.

7. The ad is reprinted in *Who Gets Food Stamps?*, prepared by the Senate Select Committee on Nutrition and Human Needs, 94 Cong., 1 sess., 1975, pp. 51–55.

8. *Congressional Quarterly*, February 21, 1976, p. 445. As cited in Henry C. Kenski, "The Politics of Hunger: The 94th Congress and the Food Stamp Controversy (A Preliminary Report)," paper delivered at the annual meeting of the American Political Science Association, Chicago, September 1976, p. 11. A lawsuit later forced the offending company to print a retraction.

9. A letter received by Senator James McClure (R.–Idaho) seems typical. A constituent wrote, "Ask your friends in the Senate how many times they dine on T-bones and if the answer is twice a week you better all ask for a pay cut, because you're living as high on the hog as the food stampers do." *Food Stamp Reform*, hearings before the Subcommittee on Agricultural Research and Gen-

eral Legislation of the Senate Agriculture and Forestry Committee, 94 Cong., 1 sess., 1975, p. 279.

10. See *Options for Reforming the Food Stamp Program*, hearing before the Senate Select Committee on Nutrition and Human Needs, 94 Cong., 1 sess., 1975, p. 16; *The Food Stamp Controversy of 1975.*

11. One of the more beneficial aspects of the controversy over food stamps is that it stimulated numerous studies of the program. See *Studies in Public Welfare, Paper No. 17, National Survey of Food Stamp and Food Distribution Recipients: A Summary of Findings on Income Sources and Amounts and Incidence of Multiple Benefits*, prepared for the Subcommittee on Fiscal Policy of the Joint Economic Committee, 93 Cong., 2 sess., 1974; *Food Stamp Efficiency*, hearings before the Subcommittee on Federal Spending Practices, Efficiency, and Open Government of the Senate Committee on Government Operations, 94 Cong., 1 sess., 1975: *Food Stamp Program, A Report in Accordance with Senate Resolution 58*, prepared for the Senate Committee on Agriculture and Forestry, 94 Cong., 1 sess., 1975; Janice Peskin, "The Shelter Deduction in the Food Stamp Program," HEW, Office of Income Security Policy, Technical Analysis Paper no. 6, August 1975; *Who Gets Food Stamps?; Report of the Findings on Food Stamp Efficiency*, prepared by the Subcommittee on Federal Spending Practices, Efficiency, and Open Government of the Senate Committee on Government Operations, 94 Cong., 1 sess., 1975; "Characteristics of Households Purchasing Food Stamps," U.S. Bureau of the Census, *Current Popular Reports*, Series P–23, no. 61, July 1976; *Food Stamp Program Profile*, prepared by the Senate Select Committee on Nutrition and Human Needs, 94 Cong., 2 sess., 1976, parts 1 and 2; *Food Stamp Program*, staff study of the House Committee on Agriculture, 94 Cong., 2 sess., 1976; and Congressional Budget Office, *The Food Stamp Program: Income or Food Supplementation?*, January 1977.

12. See Community Nutrition Institute, "The Impact of the Ford Administration's Proposal to Raise Food Stamp Prices," n.d.

13. Butz's initial recommendations are set forth in a letter to Roy Ash, director of OMB, October 7, 1974, Secretary's Files, USDA.

14. See testimony of Edward J. Hekman, *Food Stamp Regulation Proposals*, hearing before the House Agriculture Committee, 94 Cong., 1 sess., 1975, p. 10.

15. *Federal Register*, January 22, 1975, pp. 3483–3484.

16. "Let Them Eat!" *New York Times*, December 13, 1974.

17. P.L. 94–4.

18. For his part, Earl Butz was disappointed. He urged the White House to try another route by changing the system of deductions. This would have saved the government between $250 and $350 million a year. Ford decided against Butz's plan. Memorandum from Earl Butz to Richard Cheney, deputy assistant to President Ford, February 4, 1975, Secretary's Files, USDA.

19. On the workings of the Domestic Council see John Kessel, *The Domestic Presidency* (North Scituate, Mass.: Duxbury Press, 1975); Stephen J. Wayne, *The Legislative Presidency* (New York: Harper and Row, 1978).

20. Memorandum to Secretary Butz from Richard Feltner, June 25, 1975, Secretary's Files, USDA.

21. The participation rate itself became a subject of some scholarly dispute. See Harold Beebout, "Estimating the Population Eligible for Food Stamps," Library of Congress, Congressional Research Service, February 1975; *Report on Nutrition and Special Groups, Appendix B to Part I—Food Stamps*, prepared by the Select Committee on Nutrition and Human Needs, 94 Cong., 1 sess., 1975; Maurice MacDonald, "Why Don't More Eligibles Use Food Stamps?" University of Wisconsin, Institute for Research on Poverty, July 1975; Fred K. Hines, "Factors Related to Participation in the Food Stamp Program," USDA, Economic Research Service, Agricultural Economic Report no. 298, July 1975; Douglas L. Bendt, Warren E. Farb, and Charles Ciccone, "Analysis of Food Stamp Program Participation and Costs, 1970–1980," Library of Congress, Congressional Research Service, April 1976.

22. The White House was angry at Dole for his sponsorship of this liberal bill. They had expected him to lead the fight for the administration's bill. In retaliation, Dole was frozen out of subsequent White House policy making on food stamps. One Capitol Hill observer claimed that the White House took further action as well: "All of a sudden Dole's appointments are getting held up. Routine things that usually go through." A year later all was forgiven when Gerald Ford chose Dole as his vice-presidential running mate.

23. Memorandum from James Cannon to President Ford, September 12, 1975; memorandum from Earl Butz to James Cannon, September 22, 1975, Secretary's Files, USDA.

24. Brian King, "Food Stamps," Associated Press wire story, October 23, 1975.

25. *Federal Register*, May 7, 1976, pp. 18781–18804.

26. USDA had cited as its authority a supplemental appropriations bill that contained $100,000 for revising food stamp regulations. Smith ruled that the money was intended for tightening administrative procedures, not for totally restructuring the program. "Judge Found USDA Exceeding Mandate," *CNI Weekly Report*, June 24, 1976, pp. 1–2. Ironically, many supporters of the hunger lobby felt that the government could have won the case if it had relied on the general rulemaking authority under the Food Stamp Act.

27. *Bennett v. Butz*, 386 F. Supp. 1059 (1974).

28. Congress subsequently deleted the language in the law that directed USDA to ensure participation so that the department could not be held to such a stringent standard for outreach. See Chapter 5, p. 107.

29. Many other public interest activists were appointed to positions in the Carter administration. See Juan Cameron, "Nader's Invaders Are Inside the Gates," *Fortune*, October 1977, pp. 252–262.

30. "Talmadge Threatens New Legislation to Cash out Food Stamps," *CNI Weekly Report*, April 14, 1977, p. 1.

31. P.L. 95–113. See also John G. Peters, "The U.S. House Agriculture Commit-

tee: Continuity and Change in U.S. Farm Policy," paper delivered at the annual meeting of the Midwest Political Science Association, Chicago, April 1978.

32. The eligibility line was dropped to $5,850, the current level of the OMB poverty line. Whereas the poverty line previously used by USDA was indexed solely on increases in the cost of food, the OMB line is indexed on the general cost of living. See Robert D. Plotnick and Felicity Skidmore, *Progress Against Poverty* (New York: Academic Press, 1975), pp. 31–46.

33. *Federal Register*, May 2, 1978, pp. 18874–18958.

34. Harrison Donnelly, "Congress to Decide Fate of Food Stamps," *Congressional Quarterly*, February 7, 1981, p. 275.

35. "Food Stamp Changes Analyzed," *CNI Weekly Report*, September 3, 1981, p. 6.

36. This view is forcefully expressed by Martin Anderson, Reagan's former domestic policy advisor, in *Welfare* (Stanford: Hoover Institution Press, 1978).

37. "Poll: Let the Ax Fall," *Newsweek*, February 23, 1981, p. 19. See also Adam Clymer, "Public Prefers Balanced Budget to Large Cut in Taxes, Poll Shows," *New York Times*, February 3, 1981; Clymer, "Rise in U.S. Optimism on Economy Bolsters Reagan Support, Poll Hints," *New York Times*, April 30, 1981.

38. Nick Kotz, *Hunger in America: The Federal Response* (New York: Field Foundation, 1979).

39. Quoted in Steven V. Roberts, "Food Stamps Program: How It Grew and How Reagan Wants to Cut It Back," *New York Times*, April 4, 1981.

40. "FNS Officials Launch 'Deregulation' of Food Stamp Program," *CNI Weekly Report*, November 19, 1981, p. 1.

41. See Lawrence Neil Bailis, *Bread or Justice* (Lexington, Mass: D. C. Heath, 1974); Frances Fox Piven and Richard A. Cloward, *Poor People's Movements* (New York: Pantheon, 1977); James Q. Wilson, *Political Organizations* (New York: Basic Books, 1973).

Chapter 5. Congressional Involvement in Rulemaking

1. See, for example, Theodore J. Lowi, *The End of Liberalism* (New York: Norton, 1969).

2. See Randall B. Ripley, "Legislative Bargaining and the Food Stamp Act, 1964," in Frederic N. Cleaveland and Associates, *Congress and Urban Problems* (Washington, D.C.: Brookings Institution, 1969), pp. 279–310.

3. Bennett vs. Butz, 386 F. Supp. 1059 (1974).

4. P.L. 94–4. For an attempt to understand the refining and resolving of goals from the administrative perspective, see Lawrence D. Brown and Bernard J. Frieden, "Rulemaking by Improvisation: Guidelines and Goals in the Model Cities Program," *Policy Sciences* 7 (December 1976):455–488.

5. On legislative control, see generally, Joseph P. Harris, *Congressional Control of Administration* (Washington, D.C.: Brookings Institution, 1964); Charles S. Hyneman, *Bureaucracy in a Democracy* (New York: Harper and Brothers, 1950).

6. *Amendments to the Food Stamp Act of 1964*, H. Rept. 91–1402, 91 Cong., 2 sess., 1970; *Amendments to the Food Stamp Act of 1964*, H. Rept. 91–1793, 91 Cong., 2 sess., 1970.

7. "Work Amendments Threaten Success of Food Stamp Bill," *CNI Weekly Report*, June 30, 1977, pp. 1–2.

8. *Food Stamp Program*, staff study by the House Committee on Agriculture, 94 Cong., 2 sess., 1976.

9. *Food Stamp Act of 1977*, H. Rept. 95–464, 95 Cong., 1 sess., 1977, pp. 130–136. In 1976, after the end of the year-long appropriation for the staff study, the special food stamp staff had to be reduced from ten members to four—still considerably more staff assistance than had been traditionally devoted to the food stamp program.

10. The functions of the Nutrition Committee were turned over to a new nutrition subcommittee of the rechristened Senate Committee on Agriculture, Nutrition, and Forestry. The House Agriculture Committee also set up its first nutrition subcommittee in the Ninety-fifth Congress.

11. *Nutrition and Human Needs—1971, Part 3—Food Stamp Regulations*, hearings before the Senate Select Committee on Nutrition and Human Needs, 92 Cong., 1 sess., 1971.

12. A classic statement of how political conflicts can be transmuted or "displaced," is E. E. Schattschneider, *The Semisovereign People* (New York: Holt, Rinehart and Winston, 1960), pp. 60–75.

13. See Randall B. Ripley and Grace A. Franklin, *Congress, the Bureaucracy, and Public Policy* (Homewood, Ill.: Dorsey, 1976), pp. 22–70.

14. Morris P. Fiorina, "Congressional Control of the Bureaucracy: A Mismatch of Incentives and Capabilities," in Lawrence C. Dodd and Bruce I. Oppenheimer, eds., *Congress Reconsidered*, 2nd ed. (Washington, D.C.: Congressional Quarterly, 1981), p. 343.

15. Morris S. Ogul, *Congress Oversees the Bureaucracy* (Pittsburgh: University of Pittsburgh Press, 1976), p. 11. On the other hand, see Joel D. Aberbach, "The Development of Oversight in the United States Congress: Concepts and Analysis," paper delivered at the annual meeting of the American Political Science Association, Washington, D.C., September 1977.

16. John F. Bibby, "Congress' Neglected Function," in Melvin Laird, ed., *Republican Papers* (New York: Praeger, 1968), pp. 477–488.

17. See Walter J. Oleszek, "Congressional Oversight: A Review of Recent Legislative Activities," in *Legislative Oversight and Program Evaluation*, prepared for the Subcommittee on Oversight Procedures of the Senate Committee on Government Operations, 94 Cong., 2 sess., 1976, pp. 44–54.

18. David R. Mayhew, *Congress: The Electoral Connection* (New Haven: Yale University Press, 1974), p. 122.

19. *Committee Organization in the House*, panel discussion before the Select Committee on Committees, 93 Cong., 1 sess., 1973, p. 19. Cited in Charles O. Jones, *The United States Congress* (Homewood, Ill.: Dorsey Press, 1982), p. 385.

20. Ibid.

21. See Seymour Scher, "Conditions for Legislative Control," *Journal of Politics* 25 (August 1963):526–551.

22. On the structure of committees and oversight, see generally John F. Bibby, "Committee Characteristics and Legislative Oversight of Administration," *Midwest Journal of Political Science* 10 (February 1966):78–98; Ogul, *Congress Oversees the Bureaucracy*; Seymour Scher, "Congressional Committee Members as Independent Agency Overseers: A Case Study," *American Political Science Review* 54 (December 1960):911–920.

23. To most members of the Agriculture Committees (especially in the House), the main value of the food stamp program continues to be its potential use for logrolling in farm bills. See Ripley, "Legislative Bargaining and the Food Stamp Act, 1964"; Weldon V. Barton, "Coalition-Building in the United States House of Representatives: Agriculture Legislation in 1973," in James E. Anderson, ed., *Cases in Public Policy-Making* (New York: Praeger, 1976); John G. Peters, "The U.S. House Agriculture Committee: Continuity and Change in U.S. Farm Policy," paper delivered at the annual meeting of the Midwest Political Science Association, Chicago, April 1978.

24. The changes in the Congress are well described in the essays collected in Thomas E. Mann and Norman J. Ornstein, eds., *The New Congress* (Washington, D.C.: American Enterprise Institute, 1981); Dodd and Oppenheimer, eds., *Congress Reconsidered*; *Legislative Oversight and Program Evaluation*; Susan Welch and John G. Peters, eds., *Legislative Reform and Public Policy* (New York: Praeger, 1977).

25. See Roger H. Davidson and Walter J. Oleszek, *Congress Against Itself* (Bloomington: Indiana University Press, 1977).

26. Oleszek, "Congressional Oversight."

27. See Allen Schick, "Congress and the 'Details' of Administration," *Public Administration Review* 36 (September-October 1976):516–528.

28. William Lilley III and James C. Miller III, "The New 'Social Regulation,'" *Public Interest* 47 (Spring 1977):49–61.

29. Aberbach, "The Development of Oversight."

30. See Allen Schick, "Evaluating Evaluation: A Congressional Perspective," in *Legislative Oversight and Program Evaluation*, pp. 341–353.

31. Ogul's definition, which makes no distinctions, is persuasive because the purpose of *any* type of oversight has the same objective: to move administrators to do something desired by a congressman. Oversight, at its most basic

level, has usually been viewed as congressional efforts to ensure that the goals of legislation are carried out. If one is to assess congressional performance fairly in this respect, Ogul's broad definition seems appropriate. Otherwise, only part of what Congress does to try to achieve its various (and sometimes conflicting) goals will be taken into account, and the data base will be unnecessarily narrowed. See Ogul, *Congress Oversees the Bureaucracy*, pp. 6–11. For an alternative approach that distinguishes between oversight and other forms of intervention, see Malcolm E. Jewell and Samuel C. Patterson, *The Legislative Process in the United States*, 3rd ed. (New York: Random House, 1977), p. 444.

32. The difficulties in properly evaluating Congress are examined in John S. Saloma, *Congress and the New Politics* (Boston: Little, Brown, 1969).

33. Seymour Scher lists two other conditions that may give rise to legislative oversight. First, when interest builds in Congress for review of regulatory policy, and attention to the relevant agency then occurs as a byproduct. Second, oversight may come when committee leaders feel it is strategically useful to pre-empt their opponents by conducting their own investigation into a problem area. Scher, "Conditions for Legislative Oversight."

34. Mayhew, *Congress: The Electoral Connection*.

35. Lawrence C. Dodd, "Congress and the Quest for Power," in Lawrence C. Dodd and Bruce I. Oppenheimer, *Congress Reconsidered*, 1st ed. (New York: Praeger, 1977), p. 271.

36. Mayhew, *Congress: The Electoral Connection*.

37. See, for example, Jerrold E. Schneider, *Ideological Coalitions in Congress* (Westport, Conn.: Greenwood Press, 1979).

38. Richard Fenno, *Congressmen in Committees* (Boston: Little, Brown, 1973).

39. Ibid., p. 1.

40. Ibid.

41. See David Price, "Professionals and 'Entrepreneurs': Staff Orientations and Policy Making on Three Senate Committees," *Journal of Politics* 33 (May 1971):316–336; Michael J. Malbin, *Unelected Representatives* (New York: Basic Books, 1980); Harrison W. Fox, Jr., and Susan Webb Hammond, *Congressional Staffs: The Invisible Force in American Lawmaking* (New York: Free Press, 1977).

42. Malbin, *Unelected Representatives*.

43. Michael J. Malbin, "Delegation, Deliberation, and the New Role of Congressional Staff," in Mann and Ornstein, eds., *The New Congress*, p. 170.

44. Ogul, *Congress Oversees the Bureaucracy*, p. 183.

45. Kenneth Culp Davis, *Administrative Law*, 6th ed. (St. Paul: West, 1977).

46. Lowi, *The End of Liberalism*.

47. Davis, *Administrative Law*, p. 34.

Chapter 6. The Administrator's Environment

1. Jeffrey M. Berry, *Lobbying for the People: The Political Behavior of Public Interest Groups* (Princeton: Princeton University Press, 1977).

2. David Vogel, *Lobbying the Corporation* (New York: Basic Books, 1978).

3. Berry, *Lobbying for the People*.

4. The process by which interest groups attempt to draw other parties into a conflict to change the balance of power is explored by Michael Lipsky, "Protest as a Political Resource," *American Political Science Review* 62 (December 1968):1144–1158; E. E. Schattschneider, *The Semisovereign People* (New York: Holt, Rinehart and Winston, 1960).

5. See Marver H. Bernstein, *Regulating Business by Independent Commission* (Princeton: Princeton University Press, 1955); and *contra*, Paul J. Quirk, *Industry Influence in Federal Regulatory Agencies* (Princeton: Princeton University Press, 1981). On the evolution of popular thinking about regulatory agencies, see Paul H. Weaver, "Regulation, Social Policy, and Class Conflict," *Public Interest* 50 (Winter 1978):45–63.

6. See Norton E. Long, "Power and Administration," *Public Administration Review* 9 (Autumn 1949):257–264.

7. Francis E. Rourke, *Bureaucracy, Politics, and Public Policy*, 2nd ed. (Boston: Little, Brown, 1976), p. 46.

8. Hugh Heclo, *A Government of Strangers* (Washington, D.C.: Brookings Institution, 1977), p. 169.

9. See Jeffrey M. Berry, "Beyond Citizen Participation: Effective Advocacy Before Administrative Agencies," *Journal of Applied Behavioral Science* 17 (October 1981):463–477.

10. See Rourke's discussion of attentive publics in *Bureaucracy, Politics, and Public Policy*, pp. 44–51.

11. Raymond A. Bauer, Ithiel de Sola Pool, and Lewis Anthony Dexter, *American Business and Public Policy* (New York: Atherton, 1968), pp. 350–357.

12. See Lewis Anthony Dexter, *How Organizations Are Represented in Washington* (Indianapolis: Bobbs-Merrill, 1969).

13. Jeffrey M. Berry and Bill Fisher, "Public Interest Groups as the Loyal Opposition," *Citizen Participation* 2 (July-August 1981):14–15.

14. Walter A. Rosenbaum, "Public Involvement as Reform and Ritual," in Stuart Langton, ed., *Citizen Participation in America* (Lexington, Mass.: D. C. Heath, 1978), pp. 81–96.

15. See David Vogel, "The Public Interest Movement and the American Reform Tradition," *Political Science Quarterly* 95 (Winter 1980–1981):607–627.

16. Rosenbaum, "Public Involvement as Reform and Ritual," p. 81.

17. Daniel Mazmanian and Jeanne Nienaber, *Can Organizations Change?* (Washington, D.C.: Brookings Institution, 1979); Jerry Delli Priscoli, "The Enduring Myths of Public Involvement," *Citizen Participation* 3 (March-April 1982):5ff.

18. See generally Douglass Cater, *Power in Washington* (New York: Random House, 1964); J. Leiper Freeman, *The Political Process*, 2nd ed. (New York: Random House, 1965); Roger H. Davidson, "Breaking Up Those 'Cozy Triangles': An Impossible Dream?" in Susan Welch and John G. Peters, eds., *Legislative Reform and Public Policy* (New York: Praeger, 1977).

19. Cater, *Power in Washington*, p. 18.

20. Hugh Heclo, "Issue Networks and the Executive Establishment," in Anthony King, ed., *The New American Political System* (Washington, D.C.: American Enterprise Institute, 1978), pp. 87–124.

21. Cater, *Power in Washington*, p. 25.

22. Heclo, "Issue Networks," p. 88.

23. Ibid., pp. 115–124.

24. Lawrence C. Dodd and Richard L. Schott, *Congress and the Administrative State* (New York: Wiley, 1979), p. 103.

25. See Randall B. Ripley and Grace A. Franklin, *Congress, the Bureaucracy, and Public Policy* (Homewood, Ill.: Dorsey Press, 1976), pp. 22–70.

26. Carl J. Friedrich, "Public Policy and the Nature of Administrative Responsibility," *Public Policy* 1 (1940):3–24.

27. Herman Finer, "Administrative Responsibility in Democratic Government," *Public Administration Review* 1 (Summer 1941):335–350.

28. On the realities of the delegation doctrine, see Kenneth Culp Davis, *Administrative Law*, 6th ed. (St. Paul: West, 1977), pp. 33–55; Kenneth Culp Davis, *Discretionary Justice* (Baton Rouge: Louisiana State University Press, 1969).

29. Jerome T. Murphy writes that "the politics of passing legislation frequently requires that a bill's intent be unclear." See Murphy, "The Education Bureaucracies Implement Novel Policy: The Politics of Title I of ESEA, 1965–72," in Allan P. Sindler, ed., *Policy and Politics in America* (Boston: Little, Brown, 1973), p. 194. See also Lawrence D. Brown and Bernard J. Frieden, "Rulemaking by Improvisation: Guidelines and Goals in the Model Cities Program," *Policy Sciences* 7 (December 1976):455–488.

30. See James D. Thompson, *Organizations in Action* (New York: McGraw-Hill, 1967), pp. 117–131.

31. Herbert A. Simon, *Administrative Behavior*, 2nd ed. (New York: Free Press, 1957).

32. See generally Michael Maccoby, *The Gamesman* (New York: Simon and Schuster, 1976); Robert Presthus, *The Organizational Society*, rev. ed. (New York: St. Martin's, 1978).

33. Thompson, *Organizations in Action*, pp. 117–132.

34. A. Lee Fritschler writes, "the fact that Congress has the power to rise up in awesome dissent, at least occasionally, serves to remind administrators that the road to success is paved with quietly negotiated accommodation of agency policy to the views of key congressmen." Fritschler, *Smoking and Politics*, 3rd ed. (Englewood Cliffs, N.J.: Prentice-Hall, 1983), p. 112.

35. V. O. Key, Jr., "Legislative Control," in Fritz Morstein Marx, ed., *Elements of Public Administration* (New York: Prentice-Hall, 1946), p. 351.

36. Finer, "Administrative Responsibility."

37. Friedrich, "Public Policy."

38. Theodore J. Lowi, *The End of Liberalism* (New York: Norton, 1969).

39. Joseph P. Harris, *Congressional Control of Administration* (Washington, D.C.: Brookings Institution, 1964).

40. On the question of discretionary limits, see Davis, *Discretionary Justice*.

41. One of the Reagan administration's reforms enacted by Congress disqualifies any family having a gross income over 130 percent of the OMB line. This change creates a work disincentive for those just below 130 percent.

42. On such welfare efforts, see Sar A. Levitan and Robert Taggart, *The Promise of Greatness* (Cambridge, Mass.: Harvard University Press, 1976).

43. Charles S. Hyneman, *Bureaucracy in a Democracy* (New York: Harper and Brothers, 1950), p. 81. Cited in Morris S. Ogul, *Congress Oversees the Bureaucracy* (Pittsburgh: University of Pittsburgh Press, 1981), p. 8.

44. See Lowi's discussion of "juridical democracy" in *The End of Liberalism*, pp. 287–314.

45. Richard P. Nathan, "Food Stamps and Welfare Reform," *Policy Analysis* 2 (Winter 1976):64.

46. Congressional Budget Office, *The Food Stamp Program: Income or Food Supplementation?*, January 1977, pp. 37–39. See also Kenneth W. Clarkson, *Food Stamps and Nutrition* (Washington, D.C.: American Enterprise Institute, 1975), pp. 35–54; Maurice MacDonald, *Food, Stamps and Income Maintenance* (New York: Academic Press, 1977), pp. 49–59.

47. See Gilbert Y. Steiner, *Social Insecurity* (Chicago: Rand McNally, 1966).

48. See Martin Anderson, *Welfare* (Stanford: Hoover Institution Press, 1978).

49. Ibid.

50. Gilbert Y. Steiner, *The State of Welfare* (Washington, D.C.: Brookings Institution, 1971), pp. 191–236.

51. Nick Kotz, *Hunger in America: The Federal Response* (New York: Field Foundation, 1979).

52. James O. Freedman, *Crisis and Legitimacy* (New York: Cambridge University Press, 1978).

NOTES TO EPILOGUE

Epilogue

1. Nick Kotz, *Hunger in America: The Federal Response* (New York: Field Foundation, 1979).

2. Linda Demkovich, "The Hungry Poor May Be Casualties of this Year's Battle of the Budget," *National Journal*, February 12, 1983, pp. 329–332; testimony of Dr. Jean Mayer before the Subcommittee on Elementary, Secondary, and Vocational Education, House Committee on Education and Labor, March 9, 1983 (mimeo); "Infant Mortality Study Released by FRAC," *Foodlines*, March 1983, p. 2; Elizabeth Wehr, "Congress, Administration Debate Need for More Help to Fight Hunger in America," *Congressional Quarterly*, May 7, 1983, pp. 881–886.

3. "President's Budget Anticipates $1.5 Billion in FNS Cuts Next Year," *Nutrition Week*, February 3, 1983, p. 1.

INDEX

INDEX